CLOSE-UP
of
THE JAP FIGHTING-MAN

BY

LIEUTENANT COLONEL WARREN J. CLEAR
GENERAL STAFF CORPS, UNITED STATES ARMY

●

LECTURE
DELIVERED AT THE
COMMAND AND GENERAL STAFF SCHOOL
FORT LEAVENWORTH, KANSAS
OCTOBER, 1942

Published by Books Express Publishing
Copyright © Books Express, 2010
ISBN 978-1-907521-16-4
To purchase copies at discounted prices please contact info@books-express.com

CLOSE-UP OF THE JAP FIGHTING-MAN

LIEUTENANT COLONEL WARREN J. CLEAR
General Staff Corps, United States Army

The typical Jap is a runt. Five feet three inches tall, he weighs 118 pounds. He is one hundred percent literate. He is paid $15.10 a year, or $1.26 a month,* of which sum he is allowed to squander 9½ cents on himself.

He can live on a handful of rice and a few scraps of dried fish a day. He accepts it as commonplace to march 30 miles, under full equipment, in 24 hours. He usually presents a slovenly appearance, and is no great shucks on parade, but he is one of the toughest fighting men in the world today.

This is our enemy. It will be wise for us to know as much as we can about this half-savage biped whose bandy legs have carried the sun-burst banner of conquest over a quarter of the globe, from the icy reaches of the Bering Sea to the burning sands of the southern islands. "To know oneself *and* the enemy is the secret of victory," says five-foot-two General Sadao Araki, the evil genius of Japan. Our soldiers, marines, and sailors who are now fighting him are too busy taking the Jap apart to ask how he is put together. But we at home can know—and should know—just what kind of fighting animal this is that is holding the world's longest battle line, from Kiska to Tulagi.

In our effort to know all we can about our enemy we are, it seems to me, justified in giving a little to a psychological study of the fellow we are fighting. The security of nations, of men, of phenomena, racial and political, is, after all, mainly psychological. Our psychological interest perhaps should be our dominating interest because the soul of man is his greatest part. We must begin any psychological study of the Japanese soldier by making ourselves aware of

---

*Based on present yen value of 23 cents. The Jap general receives 100 times as much as a shimpei or private.

the extent to which the Japanese national character has been fixed by the discipline of centuries and the degree to which the Japanese fighter's character has been fixed by that discipline. For it is certainly to the long discipline of the past that Japan owes the moral strength behind her unexpected display of aggressive power. No superficial observation could discern the silent energies and the unconscious heroism that impel this mass of ninety million souls—the compressed force ready to expand for destruction at Imperial bidding like the pent-up steam in a boiler. In the leaders of a nation with such a military and political history one might expect to find all those abilities of supreme importance in diplomacy and war. But such capacities could prove of little worth were it not for the character of the *masses*—the quality of the material that moves to command with the power of wind and tides. *Behind Japan's military capacity is the disciplined experience of a thousand years.*

Before the Pacific conflagration started, many of us armed ourselves with the latest Encyclopedia, the Statesmen's Year Book, Jane's Fighting Ships, and other tomes, and carefully measured the relative fighting strengths of the American and Japanese armed forces in terms of keels, battalions, and guns.

We could calculate to the ton on the weight of iron and lead the ships could throw but we neglected to take into consideration the most important factor of all—the specific gravity of Japanese militarism. We did not try to measure the weight of the human stuff Japan is able to throw into her drive for empire. We missed the point that the sword is the sacred emblem of a warlike and warloving nation of eighty millions. "The sword is our 'steel bible,' " said General Hayashi. We failed to realize that the Army is Japan. The Japanese people do not merely love it, they are its flesh and blood, and physically and spiritually indistinguishable from it. When it goes into battle it is themselves translated into action. It is the incarnation of their instincts and ambitions.

To know the little yellow man well, as he really is—in camp, on the march, and in battle, it is necessary to know something about his background; because, unique among all the fighters of the world, the Jap soldier cannot be understood unless seen in the light of the centuries of fuedalism which have produced him. One must enter into the laboratory of history wherein were compounded the psychological elements that compose his make-up.

An extraordinary anachronism, he fights with the most modern weapons, but is yet a creature of barbaric thousand-year-old customs. These ancient compulsions demanded, and still demand, unhesitating self-sacrifice; emphasize the claims of community over the individual, of feudal despots over law, of death over life; practically destroy all moral values as we know them; and make the Japanese quite indifferent to physical or mental suffering. This old savagery, this inbred brutality, has been inherited—proudly, you might say—by the modern Jap soldier.

Mr. Yukio Ozaki, M. P., one of Japan's few liberals and former Minister of Education, told me: "We Japanese, and particularly the Japanese soldier, are inscrutable. The forces and influences that made us what we are, moulded us in rigid forms for a thousand years. If you would find out something about us I would advise you to examine those forces and influences. Call in History and she can assist you in obtaining a real understanding of Japanese psychology. Write down every conversation, every speech you hear while with our Army, because in this country, more than in any other, the words of the strong make the minds of the weak."

The modern Jap soldier is the product of centuries of internecine warfare beginning back in the Stone Age. Almost all the uncovered relics of that period are spears, bows and arrows, and swords. As early as a thousand years ago, warfare between the clans was unending. In the fierce battles, no quarter was ever shown. The records show that when the Tairas fought the Minamotos in the 12th Century, all prisoners—men, women, and children—were decapitated. In 1598, during Kato's invasion of the mainland of Asia, his troops beheaded 38,700 Chinese and Koreans. The ears and noses were cut off, pickled, and sent back in tubs to Kyoto, where they were deposited in a mound in the grounds of the temple of Diabutsu. A monument marked *Mimizuka*, or Ear-mound, still stands over this memento of merciless warfare.

In 1600, in a battle between the Regent Iyeyasu and his enemy Mitsunari, over forty thousand of Mitsunari's men were slain and their decapitated heads buried in a ghastly mound called *Kubi-zuka*, or Head-pile, which can still be seen today. Up until 1870, indeed, it was the usual Japanese procedure to collect enemy heads after every battle. The official tally was always made, and a formal report of the casualties rendered, on this basis. Heads of enemy officers were strung on a rope between two poles, each of the gruesome trophies being ticketed with name and rank.

It was this same Shogun, Iyeyasu, who began the terrible persecutions against the Spanish and Portuguese missionaries and Christian Japanese converts. The pages of history show no more terrible brutality, the fiendish refinements of cruelty visited on the victims being almost beyond belief. Christians were buried alive, torn asunder by oxen, thrown from cliffs onto the rocks below, tied in pairs in huge rice bags which were pyramided and then set on fire. Japanese official records of the times reveal tortures too revolting to be described. The sadism that is latent in every Japanese male had to be satisfied. It is little less vicious today among the yellow fighting-men. We ought to keep these matters in mind.

Another thing we should all know about is the influence of the Code of Bushido on Japanese thought and action, and especially on the Japanese fighting-man. Bushido, "The Way of the Warrior," never exerted a more compelling influence than it does now. As a historical and traditional ideal, a heritage of heroism, it wields an uncontested disciplinary sway over the Japanese mind. In fact, it is the supreme moral influence in Japan today.

Bushido was the code of the Samurai, who was the most distinctive and amazing product of Japanese fuedalism. All the dim tapestries of Europe's age of chivalry do not present a braver or more heroic—or more unpredictable and unreliable—figure than the samurai. When we discuss him and his ethics we again run up against the paradox that is Japan.

His code was, and is, as paradoxical as himself. As high and exacting in many of its standards and requirements as that of the Knights of King Arthur's Round Table, it nevertheless sanctioned the use of double-dealing and in olden times authorized some despicable and heartless treacheries. The samurai code of life, high and unselfish as it might be on its best-known side, was brutal and ferocious on its reverse. On its idealized side it was uniquely noble, and if the samurai had always adhered to its ethics, Japan would have been an island paradise instead of a kingdom of blood-soaked battlefields and never-ending clan strife during which the Imperial capital was burned and pillaged repeatedly, princes of the Imperial blood assassinated, while the helpless mass of the unarmed people eked out life in misery and wretchedness, with human life held at the lowest price. All this time Japan was isolated, cut off from intercourse with other nations and secure from foreign invasion. It might be thought that this security would have resulted in a complete decay of martial spirit, but in Japan, as in other countries, populated by warlike peoples, it merely served to engender civil war as the only outlet or "escape valve" for an irrepressible military temperament.

Bushido was the growth of centuries of clan warfare and finally developed into a catalogue of statutes of military conduct. In fuedal times it operated, it might be said, as the constitution of the "Secret Society of the Samurai," who carefully guarded its rules and held their secrets as mysteries to be kept from the exoterics, the common people, who were little more than serfs.

Some of its precepts were, however, made public knowledge. "Frugality, fealty, and filial piety" were the virtues it evoked in the feudal samurai. The high standard of loyalty it demanded in the service of the feudal lord often impelled the warrior of old Japan to seek voluntary death (hara-kiri) that required a power of self-command and physical courage equal to any ordeals faced by men in the most heroic actions in European history and romance.

It inspired the many instances of self-sacrificing valor which fill the pages of the history of the Japanese Campaigns against Russia in 1904-5. We read about the repeated assaults up the blood-soaked slopes of "203-Metre Hill" and we mumbled something about "fanaticism," but we were wrong. The word "fanaticism" does not encompass the loyalty to lofty traditions which characterized the heroes of old Japan and which the troops exhibited who took Port Arthur. Nor is the word adequate to describe the Stoic courage and the spirit of self-sacrificing devotion to Emperor which is the battle-motive of the Japanese soldier today.

The inspiration which steels him to the death cannot be

destroyed by traducing it or calling it names. We do ourselves, and our men who will have to face him, a service by giving the devil his due.

This fellow we are fighting is not afflicted with any madness of the moment that can be cured by "a whiff of grapeshot."

It is no mere fit of fury that possesses him. He is not a mad dog.

It is virtually important that we admit the truth that this enemy of ours is capable of religious devotion. That is easily proved. Twenty-five thousand of his ancestors endured unspeakable tortures and death at Shimabara without one of them, as far as is known, recanting the Christianity for which he died.

General Nogi said: "Bushido is what our parents have taught us with great earnestness, day and night, from our fourth or fifth year, when we first began to have some knowledge of the things around us."

Bushido remains something very real and we must recognize its continuing potency. The maker, and product, of old Japan, it is still the guiding principle and the formative force of the present era.

After passing through the mists of antiquity and the crimson twilight of fuedalism it now, in the twentieth century, emerges as a sort of trancendental moral eidolon, gripping the heart and firing the imagination of every one of ninety million Japanese, in whom the old narrow ideal of loyalty to a feudal lord has been sublimed into loyalty, unto death, to the Emperor. These are not mere words. Today every Japanese male is, in his own imaginings, a samurai. Mentally, he always has been. He has always been captivated by tales of olden times "when knighthood was in flower." He has always been avid to see romantic, blood-and-thunder films of feudal glories—and Japan produces hundreds of thousands of feet of the world's bloodiest.

> "He loves the twilight that surrounds
> The border-land of old romance:
> Where glitter hauberk, helm and lance,
> And banner waves, and trumpet sounds,
> And mighty warriors sweep along,
> Magnified by the purple mist,
> The dusk of centuries and of song."

It was Ashikaga Yoshimitsu, the third shogun, (1368-1393), who really codified feudalism and gave the system tremendous impetus throughout the land. He did much to fix the code in perpetuity and establish the warrior caste of the samurai. This Ashikaga was a tremendous fellow in many ways, and is worth looking up in the local library.

The samurai himself was quite a bucko and we should take a brief look at him, because he is the progenitor of the fellow we are fighting. They are one and the same type. He was a distinct product of his times, developing a dress,

---

NOTE: The shogun was the great overlord who ruled in the name of the Emperor. He was the head of a clan that won to supremacy over all the other clans by the sword, and he retained power by the sword. He was the self-constituted 'dictator' of his day as long as his personal army of clan samurai was strong enough to beat down other rivals for power.

---

coiffure, and customs entirely his own, no item of which the commoner could copy, on pain of death. Like the braves of some of our Indian tribes he shaved his temples and mid-scalp, but wore the rest of his long hair in a queue which was folded into a pomaded topknot and fitted into a slit in the buckskin lining of his helmet. Scowling under his red and black war paint, with his lacquered-leather armor, steel greaves, and death's-head helmet he made an awesome and fearful figure that the common folk kept out of the way of. There were five hundred thousand of his kind, and they strutted up and down the land like turkeycocks on parade, lusty to be fighting or philandering.

If he were confronted with the ignominy of defeat in battle or found guilty of a disgraceful or criminal act the samurai had the exclusive privilege of hara-kiri—and he always availed himself of it in these circumstances. Ordinary folks had to suffer decapitation on the common execution ground.

His professional duties were those of armed retainer to a *daimyo*, or provincial lord, to whom he gave unqualified allegiance and loyalty. His devotion to his lord was no less than his skill with the sword he carried in the latter's service.

Impartial evidence from many sources substantiates the Japanese claim that the samurai of feudal times had no superior as an all-around man-at-arms with the weapons of the day. As an archer he was at least the equal of the bowmen of Crecy and Agincourt and as a swordsman he destroyed all comers, including the elsewhere invincible warriors of the Mongol conquerors.

Even St. Francis Xavier wrote chapters on the Japanese blade, and the Chinese and Koreans who were oft-times badly cut up by it had a favorite figure of speech which described the lightning play of a Japanese sword in a samurai's hands as so rapid that it hid its wielder from view behind a flashing circle of steel.

On one occasion a British freebooter, with a hard-bitten crew of free lances of the sea, tackled a Japanese pirate ship, and the action was finally mutually broken off after the captain of the English ship had been killed and his crew compelled to "the desperate expedient of raking their own decks with their own guns before the Japanese boarding party were exterminated." Neither side gave any quarter.

Ashikaga Yoshimitsu made it possible for the samuari to assume a status above the common people, but it was the Shogun Iyeyasu who gave the samurai top rank in the Japanese social order.

Iyeyasu, in his legacy, stated specifically: "The samurai are the *masters*. Farmers, artisans, and merchants may not behave in a rude manner towards them. A samurai is not interfered with in cutting down a fellow who has behaved to him in a manner other than is expected."

Under the code, samurai fathers had the privilege of killing a daughter convicted of unchastity, and of killing a son guilty of any action calculated to disgrace the family. A husband was privileged to kill a wife *suspected* of infidelity. Creditors could not gather outside the house of a samurai to dun him for his debts. He was legally entitled to rush out and cut them down.

Armed with this carte blanche from an omnipotent authority, the samurai, down through the centuries of feudalism that followed Iyeyasu's rule, did not fail to avail themselves of every privilege—including that of trying out a new blade on an unfortunate commoner for the infraction of a punctilio. Later, a favorite sport of these foot-loose arrogant swashbucklers became the cutting down of the *ketto-jin*, or hairy ones—foreigners. It was some of their number who, on the night of January 14, 1861, attacked Secretary C. J. Hueskin of the American Legation, slashing him so terribly with their long swords that he died within a few minutes. This attack on an unarmed man was, to our way of thinking, cowardly; yet, a few months later, the same, or similar, irresponsible swordsmen had all the courage of fanatics when fourteen of them attacked the British Embassy although it was guarded by a full company of Imperial Japanese troops.

So quixotic were these bad-tempered fellows that as late as 1862 some of them entered a memorial temple and cut off the heads of the wooden images of the Ashikaga regents because the latter had set up an illegitimate branch of the Imperial house *five hundred years before.*

Another band of these arrogant bully-boys hacked Saguma Shogen to death because he rode on a horse with a European saddle and bridle. They didn't like that because they were opposed to the opening of Japan to the world and despised "foreign importations."

All in all, the samurai was the prototype of the Jap fighting-man of today. He had his "points," and let us be intellectually honest enough to admit them. He was incredibly enduring, preternaturally heroic, quixotically loyal, incorrigibly oblivious of all material values, including money —the most amazing idealist in all history. These were all military virtues, but listen to the other side of him, his social shortcomings. His code of Bushido did not cover the whole field of moral consciousness, and the samurai, in his supreme effort to cultivate the military virtues, did not have enough moral force left in him to achieve anything approaching social morality.

His character seems (seems) to illustrate in the sphere of human *morals* the law said to be operative in the sphere of human physiology—that a concentration of force (in this instance *moral* force) into one channel implies its proportionate withdrawal from others. Our moral force, like our vital energy, is, it seems, a determinate quantity. The samurai used up the whole of his in a successful effort to cultivate military virtues. He had little or none left for the cultivation of social morality.

Therefore, while his military virtues were extraordinary, his social vices were even more so. He was erotically licentious; he flaunted a fierce, glacial pride; he was supercilious, and contemptuous of all below him; his vengeance was implacable, and his freedom with the lives of others was quite as careless as his indifference to his own. He was cruel beyond description and perpetrated dreadful deeds without a qualm. He was quick to anger, and ferocious in his rage.

To sum it up, he was, in shining armor, what his son in shoddy is today—a prodigy of valor and a monster of viciousness. The samurai of yesterday and today is one and the same fellow.

The samurai had the legal privilege of carrying two swords. The larger one, *katana*, was about four feet long, nearly straight, but slightly curved toward the point, its blade thick at the back, for weight, and ground to a razor-keen edge. It was carried in a wooden, metal, or fiber scabbard thrust through the *obi*, or sash, on the wearers left side, with the edge uppermost. It was usually wielded with both hands and had a long hilt for that purpose: The smaller sword, *wakizashi*, had a blade about nine or ten inches long, and was used for committing hara-kiri.

Practically every Japanese officer in the recent campaigns in the Philippines, Malaya, and the southwest Pacific carried the big sword, and never passed up an opportunity to use it. General Sadao Araki, who loves Iyeyasu's pronouncement, "A girded sword is the living soul of a samurai," and never misses an opportunity to repeat it, revived this custom. The picture of General Homma taking the surrender of our Geneal Wainwright at Corregido shows the former with both hands grasping the two-handed hilt of one of these murderous weapons which he carried throughout the campaign.

In some respects these famous swords are superior to the finest Toledo blades, partcularly in balance and temper, and their quality has been a matter of national pride for hundreds of years. Japanese and foreign chroniclers tell of the feats performed with these marvels of the swordsmaker's art—of cutting through an iron bar, of cleaving with one blow three human bodies. . . . During the fight for Shanghai a Japanese lieutenant cut through the barrel and waterjacket of a modern machine gun with his sword.

When a male heir to the throne is born the Imperial

Chamberlain bears to the infant prince's bedside, on a silken pillow, a sword newly forged by the Empire's master swordsmith. The sword, symbol of potency and Imperial destiny, remains the close personal possession of its princely owner until his death.

The favorite objects of the swordsman's testing of the qualities of his blade were the *Eta,* or pariahs. These wretched social outcasts, who were considered less than human beings,* were slashed in two whenever a swaggering two-bladed bucko felt like swinging his sword at something. An American clergyman writes: "Even as late as 1870 the average Japanese gentleman thought no more of cutting down one of this sort of legal nonentity than he would a dog. I used to see corpses of low-class men lying unburied on the highway, just as they fell under the blade of some drunken or bad-tempered samurai."

Equipped with a historical background of which the above are highlights, and having acquired a working knowledge of the language, I proceeded from Tokyo to Aizu-Wakamatsu, in north-central Japan (Honshu), for my period of attachment to the Second Division, Imperial Japanese Army.

The train was filled. Seated side of me were two Japanese naval officers, both studying logarithms and talking higher mathematics. Across from them sat their wives, one nursing an infant. A few moments later she was holding the baby's fat bottom over one of the bright brass cuspidors set in a row down the middle of the coach. You could see that she thought no better use could be made of a brass gaboon that had been set so conveniently at hand.

Looking out the windows of the train as we sped along one could see tractor-drawn field guns moving through fields where farmers were tilling their acres with plows drawn by oxen toiling under heavy wooden yokes that had burdened the necks of generations of oxen before them. Later, these same farmers would thresh their grain with hand flails and winnow it by pouring it through the air from above their heads on a beezy day, while Army bombers and fighter-planes roared by.

Some female laborers were sinking a well by pulling a

---

*When counting the *Eta,* the Japanese used the peculiar numerals employed in counting animals: *ippiki, nihiki, sambiki,* etc. Even today they are often referred to, not as persons, but as "things."

tremendous stone to the top of a high wooden tripod, then slacking their ropes in unison and letting the great rock drop on the head of an ancient drill. Above the not unpleasing singsong sound of their rhythmic chanting came the muffled sound of guns in the distance. Again the paradox that always confronts one wherever he goes in Japan.

An old gentleman in tall hat and frock coat across the aisle loosened the top buttons of his long woolen drawers for greater comfort. He was evidently an important official, and a little late, in November, he would attend the Imperial Garden Party and view the Imperial chrysanthemums in the same outfit, with his garters over the long drawers, and white tie and tails.

Arriving at Aizu-Wakamatsu I reported to General Hayashi, commander of the Second Division of the Japanese Army.

The first thing I saw as I walked into Headquarters was this inscription above the door, in letters of gold:

> "Remember, that death is lighter than a feather, but that Duty is heavier than a mountain."

"That is a very old injunction," said General Hayashi. "It determines our attitude toward our duty to the Emperor.'

He introduced me to his staff, and then we all entered a room where the Emperor's picture was hanging. All bowed at the waist, very low, in silence, for one full minute. When we passed from the room General Hayashi said, "You see, in our Empire the Emperor is our country and ourselves. The Emperor is the state. The Emperor is one substance with the state and shares its destiny. Therefore we venerate him."

The division adjutant, Major Hata, showed me to my quarters, a charming little Japanese house. Then he presented me with a key.

"We have built a strong-room for you," he said, "where you can lock secret and confidential papers. We have fitted very fine Yale lock so you can leave everything with safety when you go on marches with us."

I remembered that two keys usually come with Yale locks. . . .

The next morning at 5:00 a. m. the bugles went, and at 5:30 the recruits from the back-country farms were getting their first taste of army life.

"Wan-háshi; wan-háshi," barked a hard-looking drill-sergeant.

"What does that mean?" I asked Major Hata, as the awkward-looking recruits stumbled by.

"These fellows are from the country," he replied, "and they don't know their right foot from their left. But every Japanese always holds the rice bowl or teacup *(wan)* in his left hand, and the chopstick *(háshi)* in his right. So the sergeant shouts, '*Teacup, chopsticks; teacup chopsticks*'; and they know what he means."

On another occasion, Hata told me, "Last night I ordered one of these rustics of ours to put out the light in a tent. A few minutes later I saw him blowing at the electric-light globe as if it were a candle."

Country bumpkins comprise the bulk of the raw material out of which the Japanese officer fashions the army, seventy percent of its strength being drawn from the fields. But though it may be raw in a physical sense, it has, nevertheless, received considerable mental and psychological conditioning before it reaches the army. The officer can be sure the recruit "knows" the following highly important "facts."

First of all, this simple yokel knows he is descended from the gods. That is his faith and the faith of one hundred million of his brothers. Beyond this, he knows without questioning that his Emperor is more than an emperor in the sense that Charlemagne or Kaiser Wilhelm was an emperor. His Emperor is the Son of Heaven, the Supreme Being, an incarnate god. The recruit doesn't know that the Emperor is the wonderfully convenient instrument used by a crafty, cruel, and aggressive military oligarchy to manipulate the masses to its will.

When the Emperor passes along a street, all second-story windows must be covered, and everyone must descend to the first floor. This is to make sure that no mortal is on a higher elevation than the Emperor. To all his millions, this little be-spectaled man, this rather fragile Hirohito, has a sacredness and inviolability that we accord only to the Diety. Even his portrait is divine. Hundreds of Japs have given their lives trying to save the Imperial portrait from burning buildings, it being considered far more important to rescue the picture than to save the lives of human beings. Several instances are on record where the principal of a burned schoolhouse committed hara-kiri because he was unable to save the Imperial Portrait. The army has the same reverent attitude. Every morning and evening as the officers and soldiers of the Second Division passed the building in which the Imperial likeness was enshrined, they paused and made a complete obeisance.

The recruit is also "conditioned" by influences that put their stamp upon him long before he enters barracks.

He is the poduct of a thousand years of discipline in hardship and instinctive obedience. His imagination is fired by years of recitals of the countless deeds of supreme sacrifice and devotion on the part of his ancestors who died in the Imperial service. In his schoolroom there is, probably, a replica of the stone tower, over two hundred feet high, that stands on the summit of Peiyushan, one of the hills overlooking Port Arthur. This monument memorializes heroes, including, most likely, men of his own family, who lie in the vaults under the tower. The gigantic tomb contains the bones of the twenty-three thousand Japanese who made the supreme sacrifice in the successive attacks that led to the fall of the Manchurian fortress.

Also in his school are models of Peiyushan itself, of Kikwanshan, ow "203 Metre Hill,' of the Bodai and Erlungshan forts, with their wide, deep, concrete-sided ditches which the Japanese infantry had to cross after they had survived the murderous cross-fire that swept the steep *glacis* with its broad belts of electrified barbed wire.

Without question his class-room displays a small, temple-like structure in which is enshrined bronze images of the three soldiers of the engineer corps who made a bangalore torpedo of their own bodies and were blown to bits in the Emperor's service under the Chinese wire entanglements at Shanghai. He will have seen school dreams portraying the glorious self-sacrifice of "The Three Living Torpedoes" and he will have visualized himself in a similar heroic role of self-immolation. The mothers of these three heroes were taken over all the islands of the Empire in a special train, and hundreds of thousands fought for the privilege of kissing the hems of their kimonas. Money from Japanese all over the world, including the United States and South America, poured in to buy a monument to the *"San Yushi"* (the three heroes).

At Aizu-Wakamatsu, ancient stronghold of the Matsudaira Clan, the ceremonies attendant on a conscript's leave-taking show the significance attached to the call to duty in the Emperor's service.

The town assembled to honor its fifty conscripts who were seated in three rows on a snowy white unpainted wooden platform set under a magnificent *suna-matsu* (pine tree) at least six feet in diameter. Its lower branches swept downward, almost to the ground, forming a great green canopy.

The Mayor of the town mounted the platform, bowed low to the conscripts, and read the following portion of the Imperial Rescript of the Emperor Meiji to his soldiers:

"I am your Commander-in-Chief, you are my strong arms. You shall regard me as your head, then shall our relation be close and deep. By the grace of Heaven I protect and rule this land. Whether I shall adequately fulfil my duty to the Ancestors depends upon your fildelity. Should the prestige of the country suffer diminution you shall sorrow with me. Should our power increase and our glory shine more brightly then I with you shall share that glory. If you unite with me in fidelity to duty, if you devote your strength to the protection of the nation . . . then our courage and power shall illuminate the whole earth."

Following the reading of the Rescript the Mayor read from another scroll.

"The Sacred Emperor above holds in his hand all the powers of government. Below him the whole realm of loyal subjects obey his Imperial Will. . . ."

The Mayor went on . . . "The August Benevolence of the Emperor extends to the four corners of the land. From the western shores to the uttermost confines on the east there is no being that lacks refreshment from the gentle dews of his benevolence. All are strengthened and nourished by the winds of his grace. We must never forget that it is due to the possession of such a peerless Emperor alone that the three thousand years of our history have been as a flawless golden vessel. It is because of him that it shall remain forever unalterable and immutable for a thousand and yet eight thousand years."

Turning, and bowing low to the conscripts, the Mayor retired, to be succeeded by the Commander of the 29th Infantry Regiment, who returned the deferential bow of the audience. It could be seen at once that the community held him in esteem and, perhaps, affection.

The Colonel delivered a forthright speech in which he pulled no punches. He hinted that the conscripts might have the privilege of fighting in the service of the Emperor.

". . . As the dying leopard leaves its coat to man, so a warrior's reputation serves his sons after his death," he began.

"The powerful weapons of a nation's might are not gilded helmets nor iron armour. They are the virtues of the people. . . .

"You will see that these conscripts, these sons of yours, will be nurtured by the Army. They will be given the courage that will impel them to leap like lions on the foe . . . the courage that in spite of great odds will endure all hardship and advance with the irresistable momentum of the mountain torrent that rages down the hill behind me here.

" . . . In the moment of national crisis our lives are of featherweight significance, and immense treasures as valueless as the dust in your streets.

" . . . Each subject, *as each least handful of earth*, is in the service *and possession of* the Emperor."

By any standards it was a good speech and, in its effectiveness, a great speech.

All Japanese government and, particularly, military propaganda, is directed at the emotions of the masses and the troops, rather than the intellect. It is simple, and employs the device of repetition of the same ideas over and over again.

The Colonel turned to the conscripts: "Tomorrow you will report to your regiment, but today, before you leave, you will observe the ancient ritual of your fathers—a ritual that your city has done well to preserve. You will repair to your homes and there you will prepare yourselves, in reverent meditation, for your entry into the Emperor's service. There you will bathe, and don the white kimona of the corpse arrayed for burial. You will drink the symbolic, purifying cup of clear, cold water. You will say farewell at the cemetery before the tombs of your ancestors and receive from them all the inherited loyalty for the Emperor that your family's generations have cherished."

A few days later I saw the same recruits, with many others from neighboring towns and villages, were lined up on the parade-ground to receive their rifles. Facing them were long wooded racks, filled with rifles.

A major stepped forward. "Conscripts," he began, "today you receive your rifles. Your rifle enables you to serve the Emperor just as the sword of the samurai made him strong and terrible in his feudal Lord's service. You will keep its bore as bright and shining as the samurai kept his blade. Its rust would be your shame. On the outside it may, like yourselves, become stained with the mud and blood of battle, but within, like your own warrior's soul, it will remain untarnished, bright, and shining."

He then called them, one by one, to the racks, where a company commander stood with a rifle in his hands. As each soldier stepped forward he bowed reverently before the rifle in the captain's hands, took the vertically held weapon, with his left hand grasping it at the middle of the barrel, and his right at the small of the stock, brought his left hand to the level of his brow, again bowed his head, stepped back three paces, presented arms, and returned to his place in the platoon. This matter of making an obeisance to a rifle is something new to us but it is something we must reckon with.

At this time the Second Division was preparing for Grand Maneuvers, and practically every day was spent away from garrison, in the field, by at least one of the regiments. It was a tough life. Officers and men slept in the woods, or fields, wrapped only in their overcoats. They were proud of the fact that the division lived less in barracks than any other division in the army.

One night a young lieutenant leaped to his feet with a yell. Feeling an oppressive weight on his chest he had half awakened and dropped his hand on a snake coiled within a few inches of his face. When we killed it we found it to be a *mamushi*, one of the most poisonous snakes in Japan. Incidentally, there is special significance attached to a sort of wine made from its pulverized flesh. It is supposed to have certain properties supposedly helpful whenever an officer went back to his wife on leave. The wags would say, "Be sure, Captain, to have your double serving of *mamushi* every morning this week before you go."

We ate the field ration, which is worse than the Japanese garrison ration, which is the world's worst food. The latter was usually, for breakfast, a bowl of *tofu*, or soya-bean curd, absolutely white and absolutely tasteless unless one put some of the famous *shoyu* sauce on it—a sort of Japanese Crosse and Blasckwell's meat sauce that quickly erodes the toughest foreign stomach-lining. Lunch meant rice, with perhaps a few scraps of pickled fish, plus slices of pickled *daikon*, the huge Japanese radish. Dinner was raw fish with *saké*, and some rice and sugared beans.

The diet is sumptuous fare compared with the field ration. The Japanese disdain field kitchens; in the field the soldier does his own cooking on those rare occasions when he has the time to fuss with it. Since the Second Division was in the field most of the time we habitually subsisted on the emergency ration. This meant a small tin of canned beef eaten cold from the can and a couple of pieces of hardtack. Sometimes there was an issue of rice or barley or both, which could be cooked if water was available and the weather was clear.

Fortunately, the long marches often took us through villages and the hospitable country folk would provide small portions of chicken, a few cakes, and some jelly beans for each man. Their humble thatched cottages were placed at the disposal of the officers and men even if it meant the family's moving out for the duration. For the tall foreigner —*Denshin-bashira San* (Mr. Telephone-pole)—there was always the best room in the house and an extra helping of chicken and a bottle of *Biru* (beer). Sometimes there was *Unagi-meshi*, a very savory dish of eels, cooked in soya-bean sauce; or perhaps *sukiyaki*, the best of all Japanese dishes, a sort of stew de luxe made of beef or chicken and several kinds of vegetables, the whole garnished with tasty sauces and small peppers.

Here, in the hinterland of Japan, one was reminded that human nature is universal, that perhaps the hope of the world lies in the simple people of all races and nationalities, rather than in the clever who exploit and victimize them.

The only drawback to these village feasts was that they usually lasted all night, or until the colonel of the regiment saw fit to leave, which was seldom before all the roosters in the village were greeting the dawn. At the outset of these village dinners the officers would divest themselves of coats and shoes and setttle themselves, crosslegged, on the *tatami*, or floor-mats, for the night. Perhaps they had marched twenty or twenty-five miles that day; it made no difference —they were a lusty lot and they never passed up the opportunity to enjoy cooked food and warm *saké*. If any geisha were available in the village they would be called in to strum the samisen and sing soldier songs.

The final revelation of what the Jap soldier can endure came at 3 a. m. one night when the 29th Infantry regiment turned out for a forced march. The men were loaded down with 150 rounds of ammunition apiece, plus a forty-five pound pack. An hour after the start of the march a driving rain began to turn the roads into quagmires of mud. In a few minutes, rifles, packs, clothing, shoes, were watersoaked. A chill early autumn wind added to the general discomfort. Seldom has a march been undertaken under more uncomfortable and discouraging circumstances. But by midnight the regiment has marched thirty-one miles. Then it halted for a half hour to eat and adjust packs. The rest of that night, and up to eight the next evening, the regiment marched another thirty miles. Then the order came to take up a defensive position along a river line. Before the men could eat they had to dig 600 yards of trenches. As each squad completed its section it took time out to eat a couple of *nigurimeshi* (balls of rice and pickled plums), and then fell asleep in its section of trench.

At 2 a. m., after not more than four hours' sleep, sprawled in the narrow trench, the regiment received orders to make a forced march back to the regimental area. Up to this point the men had marched 61 miles and dug in on a defensive position line—all in less than 35 hours, and with no more than five hours rest altogether.

Once again, the regiment took to the road in the darkness. Except for ten-minute halts every seventy minutes, the regiment marched until 6 a. m., when a twenty-minute halt was ordered, to eat breakfast. This consisted of another couple of balls of *nigurimeshi* and a bowl of *tofu*, or soyabean curd, contributed by kind villagers who had prepared large wooden pails of it for the troops they had been told were coming through.

The march continued all morning in a broiling sun. Another twenty-minute halt came at noon. The afternoon, if anything, was hotter than the morning, and sweat poured off the men as they slogged along the country roads that were deeply rutted after the rains. The straps of their heavy packs were biting deeper into their shoulders. The mud of the day before turned into clouds of thick dust and a majority of the men put on the small cloth strainers that the Japanese wear over their noses as a protection against dust, germs, or offensive odors.

About 6 p. m. a large town appeared in the distance. As we approached we could see the townsfolk lined up on either side of the road to greet the regiment. All the children were waving small flags and shouting, "*Banzai! Banzai!*"

The major commanding the First Battalion snapped out some commands. The commands were passed down the line of companies. The bent backs suddenly straightened, rifles were snapped to the correct angle of right-shoulder arms, left hands began to swing in an exaggerated arc, weary legs stiffened at the knee, and the regiment began rigidly goosestepping through the main street of the town.

Not until the last squad had cleared the end of town did the order come to halt; and then the order to drop packs. The townspeople came running up with large pails of water, trays of sugar-cakes, *tofu*, glasses of water-ice, and carts filled with watermelons.

"Who pays for this?" I asked the major.

"Nobody," he replied. "The people like to welcome the troops. Besides, some of their own sons are in the regiment."

The soldiers sliced open the watermelons with their bayonets; but each bayonet was carefully wiped off with a small cotton towel before they began to eat.

Half an hour had hardly passed when the order came to fall in. On went the heavy packs, rifles were taken from the stacks, the ranks closed up. But before we started there was a brief, impressive ceremony.

The mayor stepped forward, at the invitation of the Regimental Commander, and read from a scroll: "The packs of our soldiers are heavy as they struggle through the mire of our miserable town."

Then he handed the scroll to the colonel, who read: "Since we march in the service of the Emperor, our burdens, even unto death itself, are no heavier than the down from the breast of a bird."

Then all the men in the regiment chanted in a reverential undertone: "Whether I float as a corpse upon the waters, or sink beneath the grasses of the mountain-side, I willingly die for the Emperor."

Tears were trickling down the cheeks of the older townsfolk. Even the children were hushed in awe.

"March!" came the order.

The river of packs moved forward. Hour after hour the long serpent of weary men struggled through the darkness. Midnight came, and a twenty-minute halt. Then two a. m. Twenty-four hours of marching. Three a. m., four, then streaks of daylight. Six a. m., and another twenty-minute halt and a couple of more balls of *nigurimeshi*.

Then up and on. Again the hot sun, and the rivers of sweat. The chaffing and banter in ranks had long since died down. The dogged silence of iron determination had taken its place. Tension was creeping in, too. Three dogs ran out from a cluster of farmhouses and yapped at a captain's heels. He kicked them away. One returned, snarling. He drew his heavy sword and slashed off its front legs. The weary column broke into laughter as the screaming, maimed thing flopped helplessly about.

There was no halt at noon. The distant roof-lines of Aizu-Wakamatsu, the home station, were shimmering in the sun. Five miles, four, three, two, one.

Then the command, "Double-time!"

These men were actually reeling with fatigue. They had marched 122 miles in seventy-two hours, under a rifle, 150 rounds of ammunition, and a forty-five pound pack, with four hours sleep! And now, "Double-time!"

The front of the long column broke into a ragged trot.

Packs jogged up and down on the sweat-soaked backs. A lieutenant dropped prone on his face in the dust.

The gates of the barracks came in sight. The cobblestones rang as the heavy boots stamped down on them. They were home—the forced march that perhaps no other army in the world could have endured was completed.

The Colonel sensed resentment at the punishment the men suffered in the double-time. Said he: "Tired men can always march just one more mile to take another enemy position. This is the only way to prove it to them."

When I interposed that these were merely maneuvers he replied, "Maneuvers are war as far as I am concened."

A few days later when I asked about the lieutenant who had collapsed, I was informed that he had died in the hospital. He had "lost face" and probably did not try too hard to live.

Every Japanese male grows up with a psychological disposition common throughout the Far East. This is what is described as the instinct to save face. Originally face-saving meant the preservation of one's personal honor. More recently it has come to mean preserving the *appearance* of honor even if the honor itself has evaporated. At any rate, the Japanese have a deep instinct for preserving the status quo of a face and reputation which, honorably, should be firm and serene.

Face saving may be traced to the fact that in comparatively recent times Japan was a feudal society dominated by soldiers. A soldier's face is obviously victory. It is an easy face to lose. Somebody loses every battle. Loss of his face, even the approach of defeat or a position suggesting cowardice, would often lead the honorable samurai to the ultimate in face saving, which was honorable suicide. There may be a good pragmatic basis for these suicides. The torture of prisoners was standard practice in the clan wars of Japan and the suicide thereby avoided something worse. However that may be, the sharp distinction between victory and defeat in battle was good soil for what seems to the West to be an extremely vigorous code of honor.

But face saving might also be said to be merely a more formalized expression of personal pride accompanied by a great deal of ceremonious tact and an etiquette of its own.

Perhaps a word about this Jap custom of avenging loss

of face would not be amiss here. The samurai are drilled in the awesome details of the tragic ceremony day after day from earliest youth. So vividly is the technique of this act of self-destruction impressed on boyish imagination that when Jap officers are confronted with what they consider the necessity of performing it, they can meet the awful ordeal with complete composure.

I once heard the exact story of such an act, from the lips of a man who had seen it performed before his very eyes. My informant was General Ogawa, whose father committed hara-kiri a few hours after his superior, General Nogi, had done so. The son took great filial pride in his father's action.

"My father called me," said General Ogawa, "and told me that he felt under compulsion to join the spirit of General Nogi and that he wished me to assist him in the act of hari-kiri, if assistance became necessary through his failure to perform it efficiently. I was to stand beside him, slightly to his rear, with his great sword (*katana*) up-raised, and strike off his head if all did not go well.

" I remonstrated with him, because he was yet a comparatively young man, only fifty-one. But he said that he had followed General Nogi through many years of difficulty and many days of fierce battle and that he was resolved to follow him in death. 'The General once called me his beloved Samurai. Till this day I had revered the Taisho as a hero. Now I know him to have been a god among men. I must be with him,' he said. I knew then that I could not prevail upon my father to break his resolve.

"I watched him bathe and put on his white kimona and prepare the place for his ending. Then he took up his gold-hilted *wahazashi*, the short sword, wrapped a snow-white cloth about its hilt and the upper part of the blade. Slowly he thrust the blade deep into his abdomen on the left side and then cut across to the right side, turned the blade, and cut upwards. His face was very white and tense, and his eyes closed as he pushed the blade home. I watched closely for any sign of weakness, for that would have been the signal for me to have decapitated him, but there was none. He was a great warrior and a true Samurai."

Here was the commander of the 29th Regiment of Infantry of the Second Division of the Imperial Japanese Army—in the Twentieth Century—telling, proudly, calmly, impassively, the tragic details of an act of self-destruction on the part of his own father. In its motivation and circumstances the whole thing was quite beyond the comprehension of the rational occidental mind. But in its very weirdness lay a suggestion as to the formidability of a nation that has been an insoluble enigma for centuries to the psychologist and ethnologist.

The Jap officer is prone to commit hara-kiri not only in moods of spiritual exaltation or depression, or when in disgrace, or about to be captured in battle, but sometimes merely for the purpose of emphatic protest against something to which he is opposed.

Because Japan made certain concessions to the United States and Great Britain at the London Naval Conference in 1930, Lieutenant Sadao Kusukura committed hara-kiri kneeling in the berth of a train.

Following the murders of premiers, plutocats, "anti-army traitors," and liberals by young army-officer assassins in 1933, an emotional frenzy, which reached its height during the trial of the killers, took possession of the Japanese people.

Practically all of the Japanese newspapers supported the public clamor for the release of the criminals, for such they were. Millions of soldiers, sailors (including officers) and civilians assembled at gigantic mass meetings demanding pardon for the "super-patriots."

The judges of the civil, military, and naval courts involved, as well as government officials connected with the trials, were deluged with petitions totalling millions of signatures and their mail brought thousands of threats. Thousands of signatures were written in blood, and many of the petitions were accompanied by fingers, wrapped in silk floss, that the petitioners had chopped off their own hands to prove their sincerity and the depth of their emotion.

The *Meirinkai*, a reactionary but powerful association of retired army and navy officers, delivered a warning to the judges to release the accused men . . . "or else."

It would have taken moral and physical courage of the highest order to have condemned the culprits to death, and the judges did not possess it.

Not only that, but the court made the perhaps intentional error of giving the accused short prison terms thereby investing them with the halo of martyrdom as well as the accolade of heroism.

Admiral Takarabe, Chief of the Japanese Naval Delegation to the London Conference, had a super-patriot break into his office to present a hysterical protest regarding Japan's "defeat" at the Conference. The visitor then sat down on the floor, removed his upper garments, and slit his belly in the traditional fashion.

As the appointed day for the Grand Maneuvers drew nearer, the training of our division intensified. Most of the exercises had as their obvious objective the strengthening of the spirit of the offensive. The technique of penetrating wired-in enemy positions was particularly stressed. In the simulated attacks by day the leading echelons would throw themselves, face down, their arms folded over their eyes, into the belts of babed wire, and succeeding echelons would leap on and over the human bridge of their prostrate comrades. The Division Commander said, "It is easier to learn how to do this here than it will be under fire."

Every evening, whether after a thirty-mile march, or a day of exhausting field exercises and trench-digging, every soldier in the division somewhere, somehow, found water and soap and scrubbed himself with a vengeance. Then, stripped to the waist, he went to work on his weapons, carefully cleaning and oiling his rifle after he had removed the bolt, rubbing the wodden stock with the palm of his hand, and then polishing it with a piece of silk or a soft cloth. The bayonet was not neglected. It came in for careful inspection and cleaning with tissue paper. A few drops of oil were dropped on the paper, if oil was available. Machine guns and automatic rifles were stripped down and given a thorough cleaning and oiling.

He gives his weapons equally good care in the field in time of war. In China, Malaya, and Luzon no dirty rifles, machine guns or bayonets were found among the hundreds that came into allied hands. Nor was there dirt or rust on other weapons.

The Japanese officer is even more meticulous in the cleaning and care of his side arms and personal field equipment, particularly his sword. Often the latter is a family treasure, handed down from father to son for generations, and the owners of these priceless heirlooms give them loving attention.

Most of the officers of the Second Division carried one of these, even on the long marches, and gave far more attention to its care than they did to their own health. It was customary to see an officer, after a grueling day in the field, slip into his *yukata* (light cotton kimono), tie a handkerchief over his nose and mouth so that he would not breathe moisture on the blade, and then remove his long sword from his sheath.

Then he would produce a small cloth bag of very fine powder and "pat" the whole length of the blade with it until both sides of the steel were covered with a white powder-film.

With soft tissue paper he would gradually remove the powder from the blade and then polish its brilliant surface with a white silk handkerchief.

Some officers concluded the rite—for such it was—with this polishing; others went a step further and, putting a few drops of *tsubaki-abura* (oil made from the azalea bush and used almost exclusively for the care of swords) on a clean white cloth, would anoint the blade with it before putting the sword back in its sheath.

One night my regiment had to attack a particularly strong position where two enemy battalions were holding a rather long ridge. "This will be very difficult," said one of the staff officers. "Last year we were assigned to hold that ridge with a similar force. Every time the 'enemy' tried a flank attack we could hear him coming in time to move our strength to the threatened flank. At night the men moving through the long grass made a loud noise that can be heard a considerable distance."

I made a suggestion. "Why don't you confuse the defending force by having a few of your men drag long poles through the grass on the flank opposite to the one you are going to attack? That is what our American Indians would do."

"Ah, very new stuff," chuckled one of the battalion commanders, who was proud of his smattering of English slang.

"New stuff for you, but very old stuff for Sitting Bull," I replied.

Using this stratagem, they took the hill. Later, the colonel wanted to know what books on military tactics had been written by Sitting Bull. . . .

On another day, the division received notification that it would be called upon to make a daylight assault with the bayonet. The samurai's instinct for the edged blade goes far to explain what had been difficult for the occidental mind to grasp—the Japanese emphasis on, and proclivity to use, the bayonet. It is the Japanese soldier's favorite tool. Fifteen and a half inches long and fourteen ounces in weight, this rough specimen of mass machine-production cannot compare in appearance and finish with the hand-forged samurai blades, but it appeals to the infantryman's inherited instinct for cold steel and it is seldom in its scabbard. It is well taken care of. There are no stained or rusty bayonets in the Japanese Amy.

Just before the echelons were to jump off, word was passed along the line that O Tenshi Sama, the Prince Regent. (now Emperor Hirohito), was to observe the attack. a greatly increased tension gripped the whole assault force. Each company, each platoon, each squad, each man was electrified by the news. The line gave off that definite odor of animal excitement which is often in evidence at prize-fights.

So far as they were concerned at the moment, these men were actually in battle. Up the hill they went, screaming staccato battle cries, shouting the names of their ancestors who had died in ancient conflicts. As they neared the "enemy" intrenchments, the excitement heightened to frenzy. This was a preview of the real thing we were to witness years later on Bataan, when waves of Japs, demoniacal in the ferocity of their attacks, were to hit our lines day after day, night after night.

As the first wave of attackers reached the trenches just below the crest of the hill, the yell of the defenders was added to the din of simulated battle. Machine guns and rifles were firing thousands of pounds of blank ammunition. Thick yellow smoke from canisters of lachymatory gas was obscuring the ridge. Land-mines kicked up cascades of earth under the feet of the attacking infantry.

Up and over they went, the naked bayonets of the defenders crossed with those of the assault troops. A number of men received bad wounds. Many more were cut. One had a bayonet thrust clean through his shoulder, just under the collar-bone.

"What punishment will be given the soldier who inflicted that wound?" I asked his company commander.

"Why should he be punished for attaining the real spirit of battle?" was the reply. "He has already apologized to the wounded man."

Later that evening, General Ogawa, commenting on the incident, said, "It is a satisfaction to me to see such evidence of the innate aggressive impulses of the Japanese infantry."

Then we all went to see a heroic tableau staged by some members of the victorious force. One of the actor's lines was:

"Careless of the corpses of the fallen piled in heaps, heedless of rivers of blood flowing on every hand, we concentrate only upon the fulfilment of the Emperor's commands and the duty of sacrificing ourselves in the realization of his designs."

The Jap fighting-man's instant readiness to sacrifice his life has been frequently illustrated since that time. I have previously referred to the "Three Human Torpedoes" and the mass suicide on Bataan.

Another graphic illustration was furnished by a naval action in Japa waters, here reported for the first time. One of our gunboats was attacked by Jap bombers in the open sea. Her AA fought them off, and shot down one of the planes in the last wave—a huge four-motored torpedo-plane carrying three torpedoes. The plane hit the water and floated. Immediately the crew of eight Japs dove overboard, knowing that the American guns would make short shrift of the plane. This they did, blowing her to bits. The *Heron*, still circling in anticipation of further bombing attacks, approached the eight Japs in the water and threw them life lines. *Not a single Jap would touch one of the lines.* There in the open sea, miles from any land, they preferred certain death to rescue and surrender. It takes fanatical determination to prevent a man who faces drowning from grasping at the rope to safety.

Similarly, the Japs on Bataan sacrificed themselves

blindly on a number of occasions. Three or four of them would suicidally expose themselves to sure death in the open in order to draw the fire of a hidden American machine gun, thereby revealing the location of the gun to spotters for their mortars and artillery.

Referring again to the "psychological conditioning" of the conscripts before they enter barracks, the officer knows that the school and the home have already done considerable spade-work along that line.

All Japanese education is pointed to the training of the individual, not for independent action but for cooperative action. When he first toddles to school the training and discipline to which he is subjected are designed to fit him into an exact place in the mechanism of a rigid social machinery. As he progresses through his schooling the constraint tightens and the discipline closes in with increasing severity. With us the opposite is true; constraint relaxes as we progress.

As soon as the young Japanese enters school life his indoctrination with the agressive Bushido ideology begins. The Department of Education, with the assistance of all psychological aids at its command, has seen to it that the old Bushido has been codified and formulated and converted into a dynamic military way of life for the nation. This dynamism, essentially militaristic in its aggressiveness, has dominated Japan in an ever intensifying upsurge of actionism since the Manchurian Incident in 1931.

The army officer who gets the young Jap later on knows that all through the latter's education the emphasis has been placed upon absolute emotionalized faith in the Emperor, which, whenever the Army gives the word, is whipped up by carefully inspired hatred, revenge, and hysterical enthusiasms. The Japanese General Staff knows that it is not reason but emotional impulses that make men fight, and it has been careful to see that the symbols to arouse deep emotional responses in the child and the man are always supplied. By all the subtle means at its command, and that the Oriental mind can devise, it implants in the young Japanese the conviction that his Empire is divine and the corollary conviction that it is invincible, and ordained to impose its beneficent imperialism on the world.

The Nogi home, where the General and his wife committed hara-kiri and *jigai* (the equivalent of hara-kiri, in which the woman pierces her throat with a dagger), is visited daily by never-ending files of school-children, under charge of their teachers, by army and navy reservists, and newly-conscripted youths.

The Yasukuni-jinga, famous military shrine in Tokyo to the memory of departed heroes, is always thronged with soldiers and sailors, large groups of whom are daily brought from all over Japan to imbibe the atmosphere of heroic self-sacrifice. There you will see them, caps in hand, bowing in deep reverence before the spirits of those whose exploits in battle they are eager to emulate.

On on occasion I was invited to visit Yasukuni-jinga with General Ugaki, then Minister of War and later several times Premier. One hundred thousand schoolboys were assembled at the shrine, participating in a memorial service to the dead of the Russo-Japanese War. General Ugaki looked over the thousands upon thousands of youths in uniform, smiled, and said, "Thus we plant the hemp in preparation for the braiding of the rope."

During the Shinto rites before the Shokonsha, the "Spirit-Invoking Temple" where the spirits of all who die for the Emperor are believed to gather, a general read the reply of Admiral Togo, Commander-in-Chief of the Japanese fleet, to an Imperial message of commendation sent to him after his second attempt to block the entrance to Port Arthur. Togo replied:

"The warm message which your Imperial Majesty condescended to grant us has not only overwhelmed us with gratitude but may also influence the patriotic '*manes*' of the departed heroes to hover long over the battlefield and give unseen protection to the Imperial forces."

That was Togo's faith and it was the faith of all those hundred thousand. While his message was being read with great solemnity they could hear the rustle of a myriad wings and feel the presence of the shadowy hosts who had died in battle for the Emperor "through all the ages eternal." That was in their faces.

Of course the note is struck again and again, of the divinity of the Emperor and Japan's divine mission to rule the world. There are many who dispute the authenticity of the notorious "Tanaka Memorial" which documented Japan's assertion to world domination. But the credence to be given the document would seem to be beside the point when the following statements on the part of various Japanese leaders and statesmen are examined.

About the time that he led Japan's delegation out of the hall of the League of Nations, in a white heat of anger, Yosuke Matsuoka challenged the world by declaring: "Providence calls on Japan to undertake the mission of delivering humanity from the impasse of modern material civilization."

The instrument to effect this delivery was to be, no doubt, the Japanese Army.

At the ceremonial naming of the present Emperor Doctor Ichimura, the ranking Court scholar, expressed, in archaic, classical language, the present-day attitude of Japan: "The essence of ruling the people lies in the enlightening of them. . . . If there are persons not yet properly governed it is because they have not yet benefitted by the Imperial Rule. . . . If those who have not yet received enlightenment under the Imperial Rule are anywhere to be found, *they are to be subjugated.*"

That is plain enough, but listen to General Shomei Nonaka:

"Peace will come when *the whole world* is under one government. Each existing nation was produced by the conquest of many tribes, and when its central power is strong, peace prevails within it. *The ultimate conclusion of politics is the conquest of the world by one imperial power.* Which nation is likely to be the conqueror of the world? That nation which is strongly united in patriotism, has unquenchable imperial ambitions, and the willingness to make every sacrifice for the ultimate goal. In the present contest for world power Japan cannot afford to indulge in *temporary* dreams of prosperity or partial advancement. The Japanese nation, in view of her glorious history and position, is bracing itself to fill her destined role."

All such statements are reiterated again and again in all class-rooms throughout the school system and constitute an important part of the mental and psychological conditioning of the future soldier that I have previously referred to.

The young get large doses, repeated daily, of what the army wants the schools to give them. When visiting any of the schools it is interesting to note the many exhortions to loyalty enscrolled over the doorways and blackboards.

"Loyalty is indeed our highest good and all virtuous action originates therein."

"Loyalty is the pillar that supports the state. It is the very life of every subject of the Imperial divinity."

"To serve the Emperor with single-hearted loyalty, and to sacrific oneself courageously for the public good, are our natural duties. They remain unaltered by the passage of time. They are the superlative treasures of the Japanese subject by reason of which *he rises superior to all foreign peoples.*"

"We, his subjects, hold our Emperor in reverent awe, regarding him as the source and centre of our national life."

The fomative years of the child and youth are filled with daily, one might say hourly, repetition of these platitudes and injunctions. The army's objective is to develop loyalty in the individual to the point where it includes a sacrificial quality that will make its possessor capable of sacrificial service.

The army sees to it, therefore, that, from all sides, in the home, the temple, the class-room, the barracks, the plastic mind of youth is moulded to the army pattern and purposes.

The Japanese officer also knows that when the conscript reports for duty he is already, at least in mental attitude, a soldier.

His military training began at the age of six when he strapped on his first knapsack (filled with schoolbooks) and goose-stepped around the school-yard singing military songs. At the age of twelve he is in uniform, brass buttons and all,

---

NOTE: Since the day when a ten-year-old Prince Regent, seeing soldiers drilling with knapsacks on their backs, asked for one for himself, every boy and girl in Japan carries his or her lunch and books to school in a miniature knapsack.

---

and carrying a light rifle on his shoulder. Not only that but he is already participating in annual maneuvers, under the instruction of army officers, and handling light field-guns and hand-grenades. At fifteen he is shouting battle-cries as he charges up a hill to take a simulated enemy position with the bayonet; he is throwing live grenades, and driving plyboard tanks through the fields near his school. His sister is also being taught the knack of being almost comfortable in a gas mask while she chalks up bulls-eyes on the school target range. At eighteen he has already marched twenty-five miles in a day with his school-battalion, rifle, pack, and all; dug trenches, filled in latrines, strung barbed wire, acquired some degree of proficiency in mapping, and a basic knowledge of soldiering.

He has been in the field, on extended maneuvers, where he forded shoulder-deep, ice-cold mountain streams, slogged through mud and dust, and cooked his handful of rice in a little bucket over an open fire with perhaps a few sardines and a swallow of tea to wash it down.

Little by little, step by step, he is carefully habituated to hardship and danger by difficult marches and maneuvers closely imitating battle conditions, by prearranged inconveniences, and rough sports and athletics.

Back to school again, after days in the field, he has resumed his schedule of reporting at six a. m. on cold winter mornings for fencing and *judo* (wrestling) practice in an open-air gymnasium.

Watching the young lads fence with wooden swords it is interesting to note that in delivering the slash with both hands he does not pull the blade towards him, as we would do, but pushes it away from him.

We employ the same principle in the use of the sword that we do in the use of the wedge. He uses the principle of the saw, and a pushing motion in the stroke where we use the pull.

When, later on, he is using his two-handed blade in battle he adheres to this sawing principle in delivering the blow.

While the Second Division was maneuvering in the mountainous region around Bandai-San we often passed whole regiments of small boys with rifles, knapsacks, and blankets, trudging up the mountainsides under the command of retired NCO's. At other times we watched them practicing open-order drill and charging with the bayonet, their childish faces contorted diabolically and shrilling battle-cries as they ran forward against a simulated enemy.

Yes, the army officer knows his material is fairly well "broken in" by the time it is turned over to him.

The officer is well aware, too, that the conscript will accept the restraints of army life as he accepts the nineteen years of regimentation that precede it. Japan is a far more realistic country than Germany or Italy, and the peoples of the latter two countries have no conception of what "regimentation" means when compared with what the people of Japan have not only endured, but passively accepted, for centuries. Military life in Japan is not confined to the period the conscript is in military service. It is the way of life, from birth to death, of the entire nation. That is another important factor that is most often overlooked when Westerners make an appraisal of the fighting strength of the Japanese people.

The General Staff and every officer in the army knows that it is the centuries of repressive discipline, accepted as a natural law by the masses of the people, that has given Japan the moral strength that is the real source and substance of her aggressive restraint, accompanied by a pan-banging, tub-thumping patriotism and an increasingly violent propaganda of anti-American imperialism, developed, like boiling water in a kettle, an explosive force that had to find eventual release in war.

The western world has never known such restraints as the multitudinous, minute, and exacting restrictions passively endured by the Japanese people for centuries.

Each feudal ruler dictated, in detail, how the various classes of commoners in his province, man, woman, or child, should speak, work, dress, walk, sit, drink, and eat, and even think. The peasent could not roof his cottage with tiles or shingles. IIe had to use thatch. IIe could use only a minimum of dishes at meals, and these had to be the commonest earthenware. When his child was born it could receive only two or three gifts and these could not exceed a few cents in value. His womanfolk could wear only wooden clogs and only certain specified hair ornaments. If he or his wife presumed to wear a silken garment they were liable to execution. He could not show resentment at this regimentation. Any manifestation of sullenness was a capital offense. He had to be extremely careful about the way he smiled. If he showed his back teeth in a smile while addressing a samurai or other supeior he could be cut down, and often was.

He was mercilessly flogged for the most trivial and unintentional offenses. He or his wife were liable to death by torture if they did not show pleasure at the news that a beloved son had been killed in battle.

Although the penalties may be less dreadful the regulations governing the existence of the individual Japanese are hardly less onerous today. Police surveillance is, if anything, intensified. Municipal and prefectural police may enter any home at any hour of the day or night, without warrant of search, interrogate the inmates, and remove any article on the premises that it is their whim to take with them. It is customary for the police to make periodic "sanitary" inspections of all homes and premises, during which every closet, drawer, trunk, and recess is ransacked.

Even today the wife has to obey implicitly and docilely the dictum of her lord and master. The father still holds power of life and death over the family, and it is a common occurrence for a father to slay a son or daughter for lack of filial piety. In a recent famous case the judge exonerated the head of a family for such a murder with the comment: "Loyalty to the Emperor flowers in the home where filial piety flourishes."

All throughout Japanese history the individual's survival has been conditioned on implicit obedience, beginning in the home and extending outward and upward through all classes and strata of society. Pitiless suppression and ruthless regulation finally compressed and limited the Japanese mind to the point where the coercion and regimentation of the individual was not only demanded by superior authority but maintained by habit of mind from within.

In the end it was a self-imposed discipline that fixed the national character and moulded the world's most inscrutable psychology.

It is this self-imposed discipline that renders the conscript so ready to accept, and amendable to, the rigorous discipline of the army.

As General Hayashi put it one day, "The steel is already tempered—it only remains for us to shape it into swords."

Colonel R. S. Bratton, War Department General Staff, and the only Occidental ever to graduate from the "Riku-gun Dai Gakko" (the Imperial General Staff College), Tokyo, included some interesting paragraphs in his final report, which bear out my own observations while with the Japanese Army.

In the foreward of his report he says: "This report is in many ways incomplete, and lacking in the details of certain desired information. This is due to no lack of effort on my part, but to the fact that certain phases of instruction at the Staff College are not for foreign consumption."

NOTE: The ageement between the United States and Japanese Governments governing exchange of officers at Service Schools provided for unresticted access to school curricula. We placed few, if any, obstacles in the way of Japanese "Exchange Officers" at our Command and General Staff School, Fort Leavenworth, Kansas. In other words, we adhered to the agreement—the Japanese did not.

"Such subjects as Staff Work, Logistics, Organization, Supply, and Evacuation are cloaked in an impenetrable fog of obscurity—the watchwords are '*himitsu*' and '*kimitsu*' ('confidential' and 'secret'). The task of the foreign student bent on securing information is, in consequence, not an easy one. The data bearing on the above mentioned subjects that I have recorded herein (in report) were obtained in *spite* of, rather than *because* of, the College Staff and Faculty."

Colonel Bratton points out an important educational advantage Japanese army officers have when he writes:

"Since units of the Japanese Army are always at authorized strength, and since they are grouped and located for tactical and strategical rather than political reasons, there are always suitable tactical units available for the practical instruction of Staff College students in the tactics and technique of the various arms."

The preliminary annual examination of applicants for the Imperial General Staff College is held yearly at the headquarters of the various divisions of the army. It is written, and includes tests in the following subjects: Tactics; weapons; fortifications; topography; communications; transportation; military organization; foreign languages, mathematics; and history.

Prior to the present war an average of five hundred applicants took this preliminary examination each year and over fifty percent were eliminated. The remainder were permitted to compete in the final examination, held at the

General Staff College. The results of this final examination are submitted to the Chief of the General Staff, who, in consultation with the Minister of War, selects the fifty applicants that he deems most suitable as general staff officers.

Officers of the noncombatant branches are, of course, not eligible.

This constitutes a severe process of selection by elimination, and the system resulted in the selection of the cream of the officers in the army for this coveted Staff College assignment.

Colonel Bratton bears me out in another interesting point when he writes: "The Staff College is pervaded with an atmosphere of unbending severity and the most serious-minded endeavor. The characteristic racial lack of perspective, and the absence of a saving sense of humor are evidenced here to a marked degree . . .

" . . . The pronouncements of the Staff and Faculty are accepted with awe and even reverence. During the entire year of my attendance I never heard an instructor's decision or solution criticized, or even discussed or questioned. There is a complete absence of the good-natured 'chaff,' 'banter,' 'grousing,' and argument with which, in our Service Schools, we endeavor to lighten the tedium and monotony of study. No recreational facilities are provided. The officer student is required to do such an enormous amount of home study and research that he seldom gets to bed before 2:00 a. m. This state of affairs is accepted without protest."

Touching on the treatment of foreign students at the school Colonel Bratton continues: "The lot of the foreign student is even harder, because of the many additional restrictions imposed upon him, and the atmosphere of distrust and suspicion in which he has to move. In my own case, I was always treated with courtesy. The impression was strong, however, that I was in the nature of a necessary evil, one to be watched carefully, and tolerated only because of orders from higher authority."

Colonel Bratton's experience at the Imperial Staff College duplicated my own with the Second Division in another particular. He continues: "Foreign students at the Staff College are not encouraged to mingle with their Japanese classmates. They are provided with a separate study room and are even grouped together when admitted to the same classroom as the Japanese students. As a general rule, I was admitted to the same classroom as the Japanese students only for recitations in general tactics and military history. I was excluded from all class conferences, lectures, problems, map maneuvers in supply, evacuation, troop movements by rail and boat, naval tactics, organization, staff work, and kindred subjects. Such instruction as I received in these was given in a separate room by a special instructor who dealt only in dull, uninteresting, and valueless generalities. I was excluded from the trip in May to Manchuria, to study the battlefields of the Russo-Japanese War, and my order for attachment to the Fifth Air Regiment, for 15 days in August, was countermanded at the last moment, without explanation, although the Chinese officer students were allowed to go on this Air Corps troop duty.

"My requests for information bearing on staff work, supply, and logistics were met with evasions or the bald statement that this instruction was not to be given to foreign students.

"By way of illustrating this point, and to emphasize the difficulties and handicaps which beset the U. S. "Exchange Officer," I invite attention to the following questions, and the answers thereto. Apparently embarrassed by the amount of instuction from which I had been excluded, Lieut. Colonel Hata, the instructor in tactics charged with the general supervision of foreign students, told me in September that if there were any particular matters on which I desired his help and information he would be glad to assist me. He suggested that I state in detail in writing the data I desired. As Colonel Hata had spent six months at our Field Artillery School at Fort Sill and six months with one of our artillery regiments at Fort Eustis, I really thought that his suggestion might be productive of results. Consequently I drew up a set of questions in Japanese and submitted them to him. A month later I received a document back, not written but mimeographed (apparently for distribution to others), and headed, "Questions asked by the American Officer, Major Bratton, together with the answers thereto." It had apparently been circulated among members of the Staff and Faculty, and had, no doubt, afforded them much satisfaction and amusement. The following are translated extracts from this document:

"Question: What is the organization of the division staff? Into how many sections is it divided? How many officers by grade are assigned to each section? What are their duties?

"Answer: This is very secret and cannot be explained.

"Question: How many rounds of artillery and infantry ammunition are carried in the division, and where?

"Answer: This is very secret. Maybe same in every country?

"Question: How many trains of how many cars each are required to move a complete division by rail?

"Answer: This is very secret and cannot be explained.

"And so on, for several pages. To say that I felt exasperated, if not somewhat humiliated, is to put it mildly."

At the Imperial Staff College the first year is devoted to study of the reinforced brigade and the independent division; the second year to the division within the army; and the postgraduate year to the army group, mobilization, strategy, logistics, major problems in procuement and supply, and kindred subjects.

By way of comparison it may be said that the first year here approximates in scope the advanced course at our Infantry School; the second and third years approximate the two-year course at our Command and General Staff School; and the postgraduate year resembles the course at our Army War College.

It cannot be said that the Japanese staff officer neglects any of the essential elements of a well-rounded military education. His curricula at the Imperial General Staff College includes the following:

    Staff work
    Naval tactics
    Military history
    General tactics
    Permanent fortification
    Railroad operation
    Economics
    Landing operations
    Map maneuvers
    Fortress tactics

Military history trips to Manchuria to study the battlefields of the Russo-Japanese War; visits of inspection to nearby coast defenses; visits of inspection to naval bases; command post exercises; regimental duties; terrain exercises; study at Bureau of Land Survey; study at Motor Transport School; conferences at Naval War College; instructional visits to plane and engine factories; conferences at Army Veterinary Hospital; conferences at Army Medical Supply Depot; instruction at Army Medical School.

In another part of his report Colonel Bratton gives an interesting sidelight on the training of cavalry officers: "During the period August 16th to September 3d I was attached to the 15th (Army) Cavalry in Narashino, Chiba. My first forty-eight hours' duty included participation in a 95-kilometer cavalry practice march which included maneuvers morning, afternoon, and night. The instruction during the remainder of the period of attachment was carried out at the same hectic pace. I thought at first that all of this feverish activity was staged for the special benefit of General Staff School students, but I discovered later that we were witnessing and participating in nothing more than routine training.

"Training lectures were given on a variety of subjects, ranging from the tactics and technique of cavalry to the care and feeding of animals. The bulk of the instruction, however, was practical rather than theoretical, students being assigned for this purpose to command units from the platoon to the regiment, both inclusive, for marches and maneuvers, both day and night."

At this point Colonel Bratton spikes the old canard about the inferiority of Japanese cavalry by stating: "I was very favorably impressed with the state of training, morale, discipline, and esprit-de-corps of this regiment. In fact, I have never seen better cavalry in any army."

The principal reason for the fine condition and high degree of training of Japanese cavalry horses lies in the manner of their schooling. New horses, fresh from the remount depot, are turned over to the regimental horse-trainers, a corps of experts of special rating who do no other work. These men gentle and school the horses for a period of twelve months. During this whole period no one but the designated trainer is allowed to handle any horse.

At the end of this first twelve-months' period the horse is rated as "partially trained" and is issued to a soldier. This man completes the training of the mount during the following twelve months. He is used in ordinary drills and maneuvers, but is not used during the fall brigade and army maneuvers, because the latter would be too great a tax on his strength. No animal is rated as a trained mount until completion of these two years of schooling.

Colonel Bratton cites two instances that indicate the high degree of training achieved by men and animals in the Japanese cavalry: "During the course of a practice march the 4th Troop went into billets in a strange village at 7:00 P. M., picketing the animals in a pine grove nearby. At 11:00 P. M. the officers and men got out of bed, clothed and armed themselves, watered the animals, saddled up, led out, and mounted for a night march without using lights of any sort, and without making a sound that could be heard fifty feet from the picket line. On another occasion, on a moonless night, the troop, on outpost duty with the reserve in bivouac in a dense pine grove, picketed its animals among the trees, cooked and ate individual meals in an hour and a half over two carefully concealed charcoal-pit fires, without the aid of lights and without any noise or confusion. The platoon later repulsed a night attack against the outpost line of resistance without any excitement or confusion on the part of men or animals."

In their initial onset in Malaya and Luzon the Japs showed that they had prepared for years, not only for war with China, but with major Western powers as well.

Their pre-war preparations were thorough. When I told a Japanese officer in Bangkok that I had seen some of the training of their pre-war Army, he replied: "Perhaps, but you still know very little about our present-day force. The Japanese Army of 1938 is out of date compared with the Japanese Army of 1942."

Of course the Gaimusho, or Japanese Foreign Office, had been used for the past twenty years to mask the designs and moves of the Army. Since the Manchurian Incident in 1931, the Army, which inherited the status and privileges of the Samurai, has been acting in its traditional role as the leader of the nation. Particularly since the imposition of economic sanctions against Japan it has reduced civil government to a subordinate role and dominated if, indeed, it did not suspend, politics.

The Army began the Manchurian adventure without the knowledge or consent of the Gaimusho, and it attacked China in 1937 despite popular and governmental opposition.

Its brains is the General Staff, which is wholly responsible for the marvelously organized and highly efficient Army of today. The General Staff, for ten years, used China as a training ground for men and a testing ground for materiel. It was the General Staff that developed the tactics peculiarly suited to the Malaya, Luzon and southwest Pacific theaters of operations. When it comes to such mundane things as administration the Japanese General Staff leaves the Army "severely alone"—"does nothing," as the Army puts it.

It deals largely in the intangible called "thought." Its *métier* is to plot, plan, reflect, coordinate, suggest, weigh, observe. It conjectures what the enemy *may* do and what Japanese generals *should* do to meet him.

Policy in war and the elucidation of all pending military problems is its special function. It has done everything possible to develop and exploit the traditional national aptitude for warlike enterprises and the inherent capacity for organization.

It is the Japanese General Staff that made the 1942 Japanese Army the tremendous striking force it is, and it was the General Staff that directed the bold and effective use of Japanese superiority in men and materiel to conquer the great bastions of Allied naval power in the Western Pacific. It is the General Staff that mobilized every human and material resource in the empire for the present struggle.

The Jap fighting man had the way prepared for him in the Far Eastern and South-West Pacific theaters of operations by an army of over 200,000 paid and schooled professional Japanese agitators who were, until December 1941, at work in India, Burma, Thailand, Indo-China, British Malaya, the Netherlands East Indies and Borneo, with telling effect. The scope and intensity of their activities were greatly increased when Captain Fritz Wiedemann, former German Consul-General in San Francisco, assumed directional control of Japan's propaganda machinery.

During the months of September, October, and November 1941, he had it delivering hammer blows at the foundations of the British Empire in the Far East.

He suspended all propaganda activities of the organization along cultural, educational, and political lines and directed its full force and effectiveness to one objective—the focusing of the attention of 600 million native peoples on their own physical suffering and the cause of it.

It was a master stroke. In three months he secured more devastating results than the Japanese had been able to achieve in ten years with the same machinery.

When the United States instituted economic sanctions against Japan, one of the immediate results was to deprive the teeming low-income races of the Far East of the cheap Japanese cotton goods with which they clothed themselves, as well as the cheap sneakers, shoes, canned goods and other Japanese products.

When any men, more especially primitive peoples, are deprived of the essentials of living, a resentment is aroused that increases in geometrical proportions to their sufferings and want.

The Japanese propaganda machine, under Wiedemann's astute direction, directed the full fury of the unreasoning resentment of hundreds of millions of subject natives against the white man as the author of their woes.

Wiedemann mobilized against the West all in the Orient who are cold, wet, and hungry—and most of their millions are cold, wet, or hungry at some time or other.

To Japan the value of Wiedemann's propoganda genius can be measured in terms of naval squadrons and army corps.

Another interesting evidence of Japan's thorough military preparations for conquest is that for years the Army had meteorological experts assigned to observations throughout the islands of the southwest Pacific, including Sumatra, Java, Borneo, the Moluccas, the Celebes, and all other islands of the Netherlands East Indies. They were also located in British Malaya, Burma, Thailand, Indo-China, and the Philippines until as late as September, 1941.

Many of these men, including professors in the science

of meteorology, sought and secured employment as laborers on the rubber plantations, in the rice fields, and tin mines.

Documentary evidence secured subsequent to the outbreak of war in the Far East discloses that the Japanese meteorologists made particular studies relative to the beginning and end of the monsoons, their deductions being based on precipitation, pressure, temperature, and sunspot observations. The Japanese Army makes the claim that its synoptic weather data enables it to forecast when the monsoon will begin, how long it will last, and whether it will be normal or wet or dry.

In addition to the data secured and correlated by these military meteorological personnel, the Japanese civil meteorological services furnish the army, throughout the Orient, with day-to-day local and route forecasts.

There is evidence that the Japanese Army received continuous data from over 18,000 rainfall and sunshine stations or observation posts in the southwest Pacific.

The timing and routing of Japanese military thrusts into the Philippines, Netherlands East Indies, and Burma in recent months indicate careful study and full consideration of weather factors in those areas.

The staff of each field army includes commissioned meteorologists and enlisted assistants. Some of these men are university professors of meteorology temporarily commissioned to augment the permanent military meteorological service.

The Army had other "well-camouflaged" outposts of observation. Prior to the outbreak of war she had established scores of additional "consulates" in cities and towns throughout the countries of the Far East. The location of these consulates were carefully selected and designated by the Army. Each of them had top-heavy staffs, most of the personnel bearing marked resemblance to Army officers. They came and went continuously. There was a very heavy "turn-over" in office help.

In Thailand I saw Japanese bombers, with "windows" painted on their sides, landing, discharging and taking on full passenger loads, all Japanese.

Coincident with intensified Japanese propaganda in Indo-China and Thailand, was an economic penetration of those two countries. In late September, 1941, Japan induced the Thailand government to grant her a credit of 30,000,000 ticals. One week later she bought 12 million ticals' worth of rice from Thailand, using the Thailanders' cash to do it.

When Japanese troops first entered British Malaya they gave 100 Singapore dollars, in Japanese scrip, to individual natives. The same device (100 guilders, printed in Japan) was used in Borneo and other islands of the Netherlands East Indies.

Japanese ability and skill in the realm of major tactics cannot be disputed. The present conflict has provided numerous examples of large-scale operation, boldly conceived and planned, and carried through to a successful conclusion in the face of adverse weather conditions, great natural obstacles, and often determined enemy opposition.

The Japanese army has been campaigning for ten years on the Asiatic mainland and has imbibed valuable lessons and practical staff experience in supply, movements, staff control, and coordination of all arms.

Contrary to widely circulated reports, the Japanese Command does not expend infantry callously or carelessly. It recognizes the great fire effect of modern automatic weapons. The Japanese infantry are instructed to call on artillery, tanks, toxic smoke, and aircraft to soften up the opposition and pave the way for the final assault. And they are *not* encouraged to get themselves needlessly killed if tanks, planes and artillery can do the hard work for them. When sacrifice is necessary, however, the Command can call on the troops to fight to the last man and the last round or to attack repeatedly in the face of heavy losses, and in the defensive, positions are held *to the last extremity*.

At Lagusayn, on Bataan, four or five hundred Japanese troops landed in barges behind the left flank of our line and occupied a very strong, concreted position that had been prepared years before by U. S. troops for beach defense. After several attacks had failed to dislodge them, General MacArthur ordered that they be driven out at all costs as they constituted a definite menace to the whole line. When it was pointed out that the forces attacking them would suffer heavy losses, the order was given: "If necessary use the attack force to destruction."

No amount of fire could batter them out of their stronghold. Finally the position was taken with the bayonet. All the Japs in it fought until they were killed except for one hundred and fifty who, at the last, jumped over a high cliff in the rear of the position and were dashed to death on the rocks below. It was another example of mass *hara-kiri*.

NOTE: In July, 1941, Major General Edward P. King had a Japanese wood-cutter removed from the Bataan peninsula for suspicious activities. The man had been on the peninsula for four years. In the subsequent attack on Bataan the "wood-cutter" re-appeared as a lieutenant colonel of infantry in one of the attacking divisions.

The principles governing the organization of defensive positions closely resemble our own. Positions are sited in depth and consist of a number of strong points, each capable of all-round defense. Dummy positions are interspersed.

The Jap likes to hide his defensive wire in wide trenches so that it cannot be seen at a distance and knocked out by artillery fire. It also makes it harder to spot it from the air. He also likes to site his antitank guns on reverse slopes so as to catch enemy tanks with their bellies exposed as they "top" the ridge above him.

Particular training is given in all forms of night operations. Special emphasis is given to the advantages to be gained by night marches and advances as means of obtaining surprise and avoiding casualties.

On October 15, 1941, a directive was issued to all Army and Corps Commanders in Manchuria that *all* training would be conducted at night, including all marches, and movements by ship or train. All loadings and unloadings, of troops and supplies, were to be accomplished at night, in total, or semi-darkness.

Scores of vehicles, guns, tanks, and tons of munitions and supplies were lost overboard from ships and lighters. Quantities of valuable equipment were damaged. Hundreds of men sustained painful, and often disabling injuries, but for the next six weeks the order was continued in force.

This was what we would call "learning the hard way" but it paid dividends—big dividends—a little later on.

Like the old Romans, the Japs know what they mant

when they go about fashioning the national sword—the Army.

Gibbon points out that "So sensible were the Romans of the imperfections of valor without skill and practice, that, in their language, the name of an Army was borrowed from the word which signified exercise. *Exercitus* was the Roman concept of what an Army should be—a force capable of meeting in peace-time the exigencies and difficulties it would have to face in war."

We saw this realistic preparation "pay off" for them when they hit the Philippines.

They came into Lingayen Gulf, north of Manila, with eighty-five transports, accompanied by a score of destroyers and several cruisers. The transports anchored in an arc about 3,000 yards off-shore. The destroyers anchored outside of them as a protective screen against our submarines. Beyond them were the cruisers.

The cruisers and the destroyers then opened up on our beach defenses with everything they had. They used reduced charges, lobbing anti-personnel, high-fragmentation shells into the lines of the newly-inducted MacArthur divisions. Casualties were heavy, and so was the moral effect on those who had been high school and college R. O. T. C. boys a few weeks before.

Much of our beach defense was smashed by this heavy concentration of shell fire. Machine-gun emplacements and their crews were decimated. The fire reached inland and, aided by air reconnaissance, knocked out many of our 3-inch and heavier guns. Then the Jap started coming ashore. He had made a landing a few days before to feel out our beach defenses and the Philippine Scouts had driven him back into the sea and bayonetted over a thousand in the water. Not more than a dozen got back to the ships. This second landing, however, was the real thing. The sides of their transports, which were really landing-barge carriers, opened up and steel barges, filled with troops, slid off rollers into the sea. The fronts of these barges were armored heavily enough to turn fifty-caliber fire, but a .30 caliber projectiles penetrated the sides. They had heavy steel double keels or flanges running the entire length of their bottoms, an important feature of their construction that enabled them to over-ride the beach obstacles. Our beach defenses included broad belts of barbed wire concealed just below the level of the water, and railroad rail uprights strengthened by brazing other rails to them horizontally. This "fence" barrier was also concealed below the level of the water but the Jap intelligence service didn't overlook very much. They evidently know about these under-water obstacles because they drove their boats in at high tide; the curved, heavy keels rode right on over the rails and wire and the enemy landing parties that were supposed to get tangled up in the barbed wire belt remained in their landing craft until they cleared most of the obstacles.

Many of the boats ran right up onto the beach, dropped their armored bows which then acted as landing ramps, and field guns, tankettes, and ammunition carts were unloaded.

The smaller boats carried sixty men, the larger ones as many as 120, including rifles, ammunition, packs, and rations.

Not all of them got ashore. Hundreds were killed by our remaining automatic arms and rifle fire while still in the boats; others were destroyed as they charged up the beaches toward our positions, and hundreds more were killed with the bolo and the bayonet after they closed with the defenders.

All during the landing operations, of course, the enemy kept bombing our lines and it was the bombing, as much as the naval bombardment, that facilitated his landing. The first parties to come ashore secured and maintained close air support by means of radio communication.

During the night they infiltrated through the Philippine Army lines and pushed rapidly inland.

It cannot be denied that their landing operations throughout the Philippine Archipelago and the southwest Pacific area showed skill, a high degree of training, and complete preparation.

The moment he had landed the Jap proved himself the savage, merciless, thoroughly competent foe I had described him to be in my report to the War Department following my assignment with the Second Division. He has no sporting instincts. "War is a business for savages," says General Shiraishi.

Three of our pilots who had to bail out over Manila

Bay during aerial combat told me that the Japs came down and strafed their parachutes a few moments after they had cut loose from them. The Japs then strafed the orange-colored life belts which our men had been smart enough to also discard.

Every bombing attack brought bundles of propaganda leaflets which were dumped over the lines of the Philippine Army calling upon the troops to turn on their American officers and kill them. "As they lead you to your deaths then is your opportunity to shoot them in the back" was the oft-repeated and favorite bit of advice.

Snipers, (and they put a corps of five thousand of these specialists ashore), would let parties of Filipino troops pass unmolested and wait, hidden in trees and jungle-growth, until they could line their sights on an American officer.

These snipers were hard to discover. Each was equipped with a green camouflage helmet-cover of fine mesh that covered his head and shoulders when let down over his face. It also warded off mosquitoes. In addition he carried a heavier net of mesh cord to camouflage the rest of him and in which he stuck green leaves and grass; a coil of brownish-green rope with which to climb and tie himself in trees; a small sack of rice; hardtack; one-half pound of hard candy; a package of concentrated food; can of coffee; can of field rations; vitamin pills; chlorine, with which to purify water; mustard gas antidote; quinine; bandages; green gloves, socks, and a flashlight with rotating vari-colored lenses. His rifle was a .25 calibre and made little more report than a BB gun.

As far as his rations went he carried what the rest of the Japenese troops came ashore with.

When he ran out of food and could not steal or commandeer any locally he often killed and cooked dogs and cats. Whether food was palatable and attractive did not matter very much; as long as it enabled him to keep on fighting, which he often did for as long as two weeks, cut off from his food and ammunition supplies. He usually packed 200 rounds of light ammunition with him.

The Japanese posted signs, and distributed thousands of hand bills by air, offering a two thousand peso bribe for an

American officer, alive or dead. As far as is known there was not a single taker.

Later on, as the going got tougher, they raised the ante to three thousand pesos and their radio blared this bait to all the villages and towns.

The Filipino troops laughed and the civilians crossed themselves in horror at this murderous suggestion.

If he was murderous and treacherous the Jap was equally cunning and resourceful. He know all the small tricks of survival.

One of his favorate stunts, as long as the defending forces had an airport left, was to fly in at night with his landing lights on to deceive the AA gunners, and then drop flares to light up the target for his bombers who would come in. They repeated this maneuver in a naval action in the Solomons August 8th and 9th, 1942, when they sank three of our heavy cruisers. A Jap plane flew over our naval force, dropped flares, and lit up our vessels for the fire of the Jap ships that had closed in hidden by darkness.

Another trick used in his bombing attacks on Corregidor was to come in very low from the seaward side—so low that the listening devices would not pick him up, or to glide down from a great height, directly out of the sun, with motors cut.

Some of the bombing formations, particularly in the early days of the war, were led by German pilots.

When he wants to locate airdrome defenses, such as searchlights and AA, the Jap will send a few high-flying planes over at night to draw light-beams and antiaircraft fire. These planes will be followed immediately by one or more fighters which strafe the airdrome, its planes and defenses, from a very low altitude.

All of this is by no means the bottom of his bag of tricks. On one occasion Brigadier General Patrick J. Hurley, the former Secretary of War, and I had landed at an airport in the southwest Pacific theater of operations in a fine new B-24 bomber that represented over $400,000 of the taxpayer's money. Several of our P-40s were out on protective patrol twenty or more miles from the field. Suddenly, without warning, ninety-one Jap bombers hit the field, blasting our new ship with incendiary bombs. They had found the radio frequency of our patrol planes and effectually jammed their sending.

Nor is the Jap at all squeamish about giving one of his comrades "the works" whenever the latter is forced down or shot out of the air. In every bombing attack he always details one plane to strafe and burn fallen planes with .60 calibre incendiary bullets or to blast them with incendiary bombs.

The enemy is not going to learn anything about Jap plane construction secrets if he can help it. The fact that the crew is incinerated with the strafed plane is not an item of any particular importance.

He brought with him cart-loads of pesos, printed in Japan, with which he mulcted the villagers out of their chickens, hogs, rice, bicycles, hand-carts and other needed supplies. He was too crafty to seize by force. The country-folk would have hidden their little possessions in the jungle.

With every day that the heroic defenders delayed his conquest of the Philippines he grew more savage and vindictive.

On the night of December 30, I met two young lieutenants near the Q. M. docks at Manila. They were trying to find any form of transportation over to Bataan. One was lying on a makeshift litter. He had been shot through the mouth, the bullet emerging below the point of his right jaw after smashing most of his teeth. He was a ghastly and pitiful sight. The other youngster was badly shaken.

The latter stated that they were in a tank platoon that had been cut off by premature bridge demolitions as they were retiring toward Manila. While halted they were attacked by a strong Japanese infantry force. When the action started the two lieutenants were making a reconnaissance of a gorge about a hundred yards from the head of the column.

The crews of the stalled tanks began to clamber out of their steel death-traps and as each man emerged he was shot to pieces by tommy-gun fire. An officer, rising in a turret, was decapitated by a Japanese who had climbed on top of the tank. Two other officers were cut down with sword slashes as they emerged from their burning tanks.

"Had these men surrendered?" I asked.

"They were not given any chance to surrender," was

the reply, "the moment they were discovered they were killed."

Everywhere he struck the Jap's tactics were characterized by speed, deception, and the use of modern automatic weapons. Like our late lamented gangsters he is partial to the tommy-gun. It is actually a light machine-gun that can be fired from the hip when supported by a sling over the shoulder. It is gas-operated, magazine-fed, and air-cooled and can be adjusted to fire automatically or semi-automatically. It also has a bayonet attachment. Its calibre is 6.5-mm (0.256 in.) which makes it possible for the individual soldier to carry a couple of hundred rounds of its light-weight ammunition.

The Japanese infantry is also armed with a heavy machine gun, 7.7-mm (0.303) calibre, of the Hotchkiss type. It is air-cooled, has a special mounting that makes it possible to use it against aircraft, and the gun and its tripod can be packed on one horse. Another horse carries four boxes of ammunition. This gun stood up very well to severe fighting conditions in Malaya and Luzon. Three to four thousand rounds of continuous fire can be delivered without its becoming over-heated.

Two weapons that were used with deadly and demoralizing effect on the Philippine Army, particularly in the fighting on Bataan, were the 81-mm and the 90-mm mortars. They both throw a very destructive anti-personnel shell and the Japanese employed over five hundred of these on a twenty-mile front night and day.

The great advantage that the use of these mortars gave the Japanese in the Malay and Philippine fighting was that they could be used in swampy and jungle country where firm earth for field artillery platforms could not be found. Most of the time wooden ramps had to be carried along or constructed on the spot in order to get field guns off the roads and across deep ditches to firing positions. The field guns, too, required towing while the Japanese infantry could take their mortars with them wherever they went.

The Jap had field guns when and where he thought them necessary. One, a new 88-mm howitzer, is one of the best guns available for the type of country in which it was used.

They also have a new, improved 75-mm field gun with an effective range of over 10,000 yards.

They even had huge railroad guns of 240-mm. It fired a 450-pound projectile and in the final stages of the siege of our forts in Manila Bay the Japs were hurling over a thousand of these projectiles a day against Fort Hughes, Fort Drum and Fort Mills. At the same time they were delivering as many as fifty air raids a day against Corregidor.

They also have a very good 75-mm antiaircraft gun that has a horizontal range of over 15,000 yards and a vertical range of 33,000 feet. It could reach up 9,000 feet higher than any of the AA guns we had on Corregidor.

Their 20-mm AA gun is a gem. It is a modified Oerlikon, originally designed and manufactured in Switzerland. It can fire 120 rounds per minute, has a horizontal range of 5,500 yards and a certical range of 13,000 feet.

Some of their other guns appear crude in comparison with ours but General Ogawa once said to me, "You Americans are perfectionists. Everything has to be built like a watch. Your 37-mm infantry accompanying gun can shoot three times as far as your men can see to aim it and it can't 'accompany' unless there's a truck around to pull it. It costs $4,000 and our 37-mm, which will do any job the infantry can hand it, costs $90. It may look like a stovepipe on wheels compared with yours, but we can turn out forty or more for the price of one of your fancy jobs." I think he had something there.

The Japs also use a concrete bomb consisting of two steel walls with the annular space filled with a very slow-fixing concrete. Slugs of half-inch diameter reinforcing rods are mixed in with the concrete which is as hard as flint after it "sets." This bomb is used primarily as an anti-personnel bomb.

Their incendiary bombs were filled with black rubber impregnated with phosphorus. Water would extinguish the pellets but they would re-ignite up to twelve hours after the bomb burst.

How they love to pour it on when they have air superiority! Coming down from Lingayen and all during the long-drawn-out struggle on Bataan and Corregidor they bombed and bombed and bombed, night and day, day after day, week after week, month after month. Twenty-four hours a day our men were subjected to its cumulative effect on the human nervous system. Tension, horror, apprehension filled every hour for the stoutest heart.

The Creation of Japan's National Army

After the Restoration, plans were laid for the creation of a new national army, owing allegiance to the Emperor instead of feudal lords. The handful of designing and ambitious empiricists who even then had Japan's "ultimate destiny" in mind, made sure that under the new constitution Army and Navy leaders would have the privilege and the right of direct access to the Emperor. They do not have to seek the consent of the prime minister. They can block the formation of a cabinet or force its fall by withholding or withdrawing their respective ministers.

If the Diet does not approve their demands for funds they can obtain them by Imperial sanction.

Japan did not come to a national army until she was confronted with the peril of Western aggression following Commodore Perry's visits. At once it became apparent that the supreme danger demanded the liquidation of the kingdoms of the various daimyos, the abolition of feudalism, and the fusing of the state into one coherent entity capable of immediate, coordinated action in time of national emergency. This meant the surrender by the daimyos of all their powers and the centering of all authority in the divine Emperor. Henceforth loyalty to the Son of Heaven should terminate the feudal duty of obedience to the territorial lord.

The designers of the new Japan were too wise to scrap the old national religion of loyalty. They recognized it as a national heritage of incalculable worth. It represented a moral power with which they could work miracles and achieve tremendous ends. So they did not destroy it but rather converted it to their own purposes and made it the new national obligation of devotion and duty in the Emperor's service.

In their planning of the new army, therefore, they

sought the elimination of the antiquated samurai *system* but the retention of the samurai *spirit*.

They envisioned an army drawn from all sections of the Empire, inculcated with a deeper, broader patriotism and made one hundred percent literate by compulsory education.

In 1870 the new army came into being with the organization of four regiments of infantry.

When the Emperor opened its ranks to all, regardless of class or position in the social scale, the privilege of enlistment came to the peasant boy as an emancipation from serfdom and a patent of nobility conferred on him by the graciousness of Imperial divinity.

Now the meanest man in the village could be a samurai.

In 1877 the soldiers of the new Imperial Army were pitted against the armed retainers of General Saigo in the Satsuma rebellion and the samurai of a dying feudalism went down before the bayonets of the Emperor's "commoners."

That victory endowed every man in the new Army with faith in it and himself.

His was the only army in the history of Asia, if not in the world, in which every soldier could read and write—*because he had received the benefits of compulsory education in public schools organized and staffed by American teachers.*

The physical and mental training begun in the school was continued in the barracks. His body was built up by better food, scientific exercise, compulsory hygiene and regular habits. His life was enriched and expanded by new friendships and wider mental horizons. The lowly peasant who could never have hoped to look beyond his rice field and hibachi* could now get a glimpse of the world as he marched with his wondering fellows likewise emancipated from the slavery of the rice-paddy, the fishing-boat, and the coastal junk.

He entered a new world in which he was guarded against disease and in which he grew in stature, appearance and character—a world that he had never dreamed of until it was his privilege to enter the service of his Emperor.

---

* Hibachi—a large brass or iron urn in which charcoal is burned for cooking, and heating the home.

He had always known that the cherry blossoms, falling in their prime, symbolized the voluntary death of the warrior for his country.

"What is the spirit of Yamato* but the mountain cherry fragrant under the morning sun."

Now he himself was the warrior and when he died in battle his soul could join the hosts of the Kami† in the Shokonsha, the Pantheon of the Gods.

There is one thing about the Japanese Army that its own General Staff is explicit on. War is no place for finer sensibilities and tender emotions, or the observance of niceties. In one of their staff manuals they quote Bismarck's "Fuerstenpolitik:"

"Whenever war breaks out terrorism becomes a necessary military principle."

The frequent quotations from the German that appear in Japanese military text books and training manuals serve as reminders that the modern Japanese Army was created by Germans and modeled after the German military machine.

After a brief period of experimentation with the French Army organization the Japanese finally decided to adopt the German pattern. She copied it as closely as a photostat copies the original. All of her military regulations and text books were translated almost verbatim from the German and the officers of the Second Division told me that the deployment of the Corps of which the Division formed a part was precisely that of a German Army Corps and that it was supervised, though not directed, by German staff officers.

I was interested in discovering, too, that over half of the staff of the Second Division spoke German and were graduates of German military schools, including General Hayashi himself who had just completed a course of study at the German General Staff College. I found all the officers, with two exceptions, great admirers of the German Army.

The mutual admiration and close liaison between the

---

* The word "Yamato," in reference to 2,500 years of development of national sentiment and ideals, has a spiritual connotation.
  † Kami—spirits of the dead fallen in battle, literally "gods of war."

German and the Japanese military minds was interrupted only briefly during the last war.

In the campaigns in Malaya, the Philippines, and the southwest Pacific there were constantly recurring evidences of German participation in the operations in the form of technicians, aviation pilots, pilot instructors, and staff advisers.

Incidentally, the Japanese campaign in Malaya was featured by the presence of an old "Hachiman Sama"* or god of war, in the person of Lieutenant General Senjiro Shirishi.

Hearing of it reminded me of the day I saw four venerable old patriarchs attending a staff conference of the Second Division.

"Who are they and what are they doing here?" I asked.

"They are old retired generals of the Russo-Japanese war," replied Colonel Sato. "We like them to see the training of the Division and to have their observations: You know, 'Chié no saké wa furui taru ni aru'." (The wine of wisdom comes in old casks.)

Anyway, from the account given by a wounded Jap officer prisoner it seems that General Shiraishi was brought to the scene of the Malaya struggle for purposes of morale. Eighty-nine years old, unable to walk, carried about in a litter, beloved by all officers who had learned under him at the Toyama Gakko, famous school of physical and moral education, he was to fill the role of a symbol of past glories and harbinger of victories to come, but nothing more than that. Carried about, like an Ark of the Covenant, he was to be seen and not heard.

But the patriarch stole the show.

Partly to please the old man's vanity, partly to pay the deference that the Japanese extend to age, the Army staff would gather around him in the evening. He would listen to the recital of the achievements and problems of the day. Then he would offer his solutions to difficulties that confounded the staff. They were usually better than their own.

On one occasion he recommended a novel application of air power! His solution solved a problem that had baffled younger minds for days.

He was not, at any time, in actual command of troops.

---

* Usa Hachiman is the Japanese God of War.

But he possessed the authority of enormous prestige that increased with the repeated evidences of his profound wisdom.

At the end of the campaign the old Samurai—venerable symbol of victory—was carried over the causeway from Johore in triumph into Singapore.

The Jap officer, when it comes to taking the best of what other armies have to offer in instruction, doesn't miss a trick. If thoroughness, long hours of hard work, attention to detail, study, and an eagerness to assimilate, and improve upon, mean anything, then he is among the world's best in his profession.

His genius lies in his ability to convert knowledge gained from outside sources, into working principles. Herein lies the potency to excel his teachers. Little does he invent but mightily does he adapt.

The Japanese General Staff has taken particular care to exploit every field of knowledge to increase the efficiency and striking power of the machine they have built for conquest. Japanese discipline may be rigid but the Japanese military mind, contrary to general opinion, possesses an amazing elasticity and receptivity. It is always ready to receive, adapt, improve and use the best that other minds produce.

The Japanese officer may not be the equal of our artillery officers in technical knowledge, but he can still do a very workmanlike job under the most difficult and discouraging conditions. No angle of his training is neglected.

Last fall I met three senior Japanese officers (whom I had known years before in Japan) in the wilds of northern Thailand.

NOTE: In a report to the War Department, Colonel Clear wrote: "The thoroughness of Japanese preparations —moral, physical, and material—and the deep studies of the Japanese General Staff who recognized that new tactical and strategical conditions must be met by utilizing the developments of modern science that created them—were positive factors contributing to the extraordinary successes gained by Japanese arms in the field.

"Are you on a hunting trip?" I asked.

"Oh, no," one replied, "we are just learning geography

through the soles of our boots." Which meant that they were making a detailed reconnaissance of the jungle paths and trails that they were going to lead their regiments over on the march to Singapore a few weeks later.

A fourth in the group was introduced to me as a Major Tachibana.

"I have known a number of Japanese officers by the name of Tachibana,' I observed.

"*Oni ni ko takusan,*" ("the devil has many children"), one of the others quipped. Major Tachibana showed keen displeasure at this sally and I recalled that Doctor Nitobe, one of Japan's great liberals, had once told me that the Japanese were supersensitive because they had no sense of humor. Looking at the resentment showing on Tachibana's sullen face I could believe it. They seldom laugh at jokes that in any way reflect upon themselves.

On another occasion two unkempt fellows in dirty Chinese clothes were walking in the grounds of the Oriental Hotel, Bangkok, on the banks of the Chao Pia Me Nom ("Mother of Waters"). A few moments later they were joined by Japansee officers in mufti who were stopping at the hotel. A closer look and it was evident that the soiled pair, talking Japanese with the others, were army officers on a confidential assignment. They, too, were "learning geography through the soles of their boots"—the geography of the other fellow's country.

As far back as 1887, Viscount Tani, one of Japan's most fanatical and narrow chauvinists, advised: "Make our country secure by military preparation * * * and then wait for the time of the confusion of Europe which must come eventually, sooner or later. Such a development will agitate the nations of the Orient as well, and thence will come our opportunity to dominate the Orient. When the storm clouds "gather in the West the war drums begin to beat in the East."

He also told our Minister at that time that our nation had gone soft and that we had a contempt for the fighting man that some day would prove fatal to us. He said we had no fighting force worthy to be dignified by the name of army and he quoted the lines of a minor ecclesiastical poet of England who died 300 years ago:

"Our God and soldier we alike adore,
When at the brink of ruin, not before;
After deliverance both alike requited,
Our God forgotten and our soldiers slighted."

Japan has won some great victories. Within four months after Pearl Harbor she had acquired a new economic empire, perhaps the richest prize that ever fell to conquest.

NOTE: In 1887 our army had a total combat strength of 18,000 men—less than the police force of New York City. In British Malaya she won a region that produces half a million metric tons of rubber annually, and a million and a quarter tons of iron ore, and large quantities of tin. In the Netherlands East Indies and British Borneo she took an area with an annual production of eight million tons of oil and a half million tons of rubber. In Thailand she won agricultural riches enough to glut her with rice and other food staples. In the Philippines she secured an inexhaustible supply of hard woods and large deposits of gold and other metals. An inventory of the spoils shows the bandy-legged Japanese trooper to have garnered incalculably more in six months than Hitler's legions have won in all their conquests.

For years a vital element in our strategy was the cutting off of Japan from the essential materials of war. The shoe is now on the other foot.

Japan admittedly has great strength. Prior to the outbreak of the present conflict, her success in previous wars and her astute diplomatic victories had rendered her almost impregnable to direct attack. Ten thousand miles of salt water lie between her and Europe. The United States is five thousand miles away, with fifty million square miles of watery waste between our fleet bases and her shores. Thus, most of the Pacific ocean stands as her guardian of safety from any direct attack by sea. In addition, since her recent conquests, she has built a solid block of empire from the Bering to the Banda seas. The islands of her Empire chain cover the sea approaches to eastern Asia from Vladivostok to Singapore, and the Malay archipelago is not only a bridge to the Indies but a barrier between the Pacific and the Indian Oceans. We have not only lost Corregidor,

Cavite, Hongkong, Batavia, Rangoon, Singapore and Sourabaya, the great bases of the far western Pacific and southeast Asia, but Japan has gained them.

To the east of the Empire proper lie the outpost defenses of the Marshalls, Bonins, Carolines and Marianas, with fifty-two fortified points that include air and submarine bases in which land-based aviation and the wolves of the sea lurk in comparative safety awaiting the opportunity to strike at highly vulnerable surface prey.

Her ninety-five divisions comprise a tough, seasoned and well-organized force, flushed by tremendous victories.

Her merchant marine totals six million tons, next in size to ours, and her fleet is the third largest in the world. Our naval officers who have faced some of its units attest to the excellence of its gunnery.

The spirit of *"Yamato-damashii,"* of loyalty and martial ardor, which possesses her, unites all Japanese in a common bond of patriotic fervor.

Beyond this she has the cult of Emperor-worship, based on the national belief in the divinity, infallibility and invincibility of the Son of Heaven.

But Japan has no magic formula for success. She has merely brought the crushing reality of greater power against her opponents. She, herself, has not yet been confronted by superior force—the only reality that total war recognizes.

Japan proved, in her previous wars, that she possesses a supreme aptitude for war, as well as a stoic valor and a capacity for self-immolation upon the altar of country.

The Japanese Army is a powerful, tough, well-organized force (of 95 combat divisions) that has demonstrated beyond any doubt its ability to keep the field under the most adverse conditions. Its common soldiers have endured privations, starvations and hardships that would emasculate the resistance of a western-standard army in six months. They have a well-nigh phenomenal skill in fighting in mountain and jungle country. They have a mastery of offensive fighting that can be acquired only with the expenditure of countless lives.

It is an army of veterans, hardened and blooded by ten years of intermittent warfare in China. It knows the business of war, the small tricks of survival, the cunning, the hard work, and the pleasures of victory.

It will take all of our man-power and industrial production and moral strength to defeat this Army.

We have just entered the opening phase of the most sanguinary racial conflict that has ever convulsed the world.

www.ingramcontent.com/pod-product-compliance
Lightning Source LLC
Chambersburg PA
CBHW061512040426
42450CB00008B/1580